Third Workshop on Privacy in Natural Language Processing (PrivateNLP 2021)

Online
11 June 2021

ISBN: 978-1-7138-3026-9

Printed from e-media with permission by:

Curran Associates, Inc.
57 Morehouse Lane
Red Hook, NY 12571

Some format issues inherent in the e-media version may also appear in this print version.

Association for Computational Linguistics
209 N. Eighth Street
Stroudsburg, Pennsylvania 18360

Phone: 1-570-476-8006
Fax: 1-570-476-0860

acl@aclweb.org

Additional copies of this publication are available from:

Curran Associates, Inc.
57 Morehouse Lane
Red Hook, NY 12571 USA
Phone: 845-758-0400
Fax: 845-758-2633
Email: curran@proceedings.com
Web: www.proceedings.com

PrivateNLP 2021

The Third Workshop on Privacy in Natural Language Processing

Proceedings of the Workshop

June 11, 2021

Introduction

The PrivateNLP workshop aims to bring together practitioners and researchers from academia and industry to discuss the challenges and approaches to designing, building, verifying, and testing privacy preserving systems in the context of Natural Language Processing.

This year, the workshop accepted 7 papers and one non-archival paper. These accepted papers cover federated learning, text perturbation mechanisms, privacy preserving language models, and secure multiparty computation.

We have 2 invited speakers: Travis Breaux (Carnegie Mellon University) and Adam Dziedzic (Vector Institute and The University of Toronto).

We would like to thank the Program Committee members who kindly reviewed the submissions, as well as the invited speakers, and the workshop co-organizers, Oluwaseyi Feyisetan (Amazon, USA), Sepideh Ghanavati (University of Maine, USA), Shervin Malmasi (Amazon, USA), and Patricia Thaine (University of Toronto, Canada).

Organizing Committee

Oluwaseyi Feyisetan, Amazon (USA)
Sepideh Ghanavati, University of Maine (USA)
Shervin Malmasi, Amazon (USA)
Patricia Thaine, University of Toronto (Canada)

Program Committee

Aleksei Triastcyn (Ecole Polytechnique Federale de Lausanne)
Andreas Nautsch (EURECOM)
Asma Eidhah Aloufi (Rochester Institute of Technology)
Balazs Pejo (Budapest University of Technology and Economics)
Benjamin Zi Hao Zhao (University of New South Wales)
Briland Hitaj (SRI International)
Christian Weinert (Technische Universitat Darmstadt)
Congzheng Song (Apple)
Dinusha Vatsalan (Data61-CSIRO)
Eleftheria Makri (Saxion University)
Fang Liu (University of Notre Dame)
Gerald Penn (University of Toronto)
Isar Nejadgholi (National Research Council Canada)
Jamie Hayes (University College London)
Liwei Song (Princeton)
Mohamed Abdalla (University of Toronto)
Natasha Fernandes (Macquarie University)
Sai Teja Peddinti (Google)
Shomir Wilson (Pennsylvania State University)
Tom Diethe (Amazon)
Travis Breaux (Carnegie Mellon University)
Xavier Ferrer (King's College London)

Invited Speakers

Adam Dziedzic (Vector Institute and The University of Toronto)
Travis Breaux (Carnegie Mellon University)

Table of Contents

Conference Program

Understanding Unintended Memorization in Language Models Under Federated Learning
Om Dipakbhai Thakkar, Swaroop Ramaswamy, Rajiv Mathews and Francoise Beaufays

On a Utilitarian Approach to Privacy Preserving Text Generation
Zekun Xu, Abhinav Aggarwal, Oluwaseyi Feyisetan and Nathanael Teissier

Learning and Evaluating a Differentially Private Pre-trained Language Model
Shlomo Hoory, Amir Feder, Avichai Tendler, Alon Cohen, Sofia Erell, Itay Laish, Hootan Nakhost, Uri Stemmer, Ayelet Benjamini, Avinatan Hassidim and Yossi Matias

An Investigation towards Differentially Private Sequence Tagging in a Federated Framework
Abhik Jana and Chris Biemann

A Privacy-Preserving Approach to Extraction of Personal Information through Automatic Annotation and Federated Learning
Rajitha Hathurusinghe, Isar Nejadgholi and Miodrag Bolic

Using Confidential Data for Domain Adaptation of Neural Machine Translation
Sohyung Kim, Arianna Bisazza and Fatih Turkmen

Private Text Classification with Convolutional Neural Networks
Samuel Adams, David Melanson and Martine De Cock

Understanding Unintended Memorization in Language Models Under Federated Learning

Om Thakkar and **Swaroop Ramaswamy** and **Rajiv Mathews** and **Françoise Beaufays**
Google LLC,
Mountain View, CA, U.S.A.
{omthkkr, swaroopram, mathews, fsb} @google.com

Abstract

Recent works have shown that language models (LMs), e.g., for next word prediction (NWP), have a tendency to memorize rare or unique sequences in the training data. Since useful LMs are often trained on sensitive data, it is critical to identify and mitigate such *unintended* memorization. Federated Learning (FL) has emerged as a novel framework for large-scale distributed learning tasks. It differs in many aspects from the well-studied *central learning* setting where all the data is stored at the central server, and minibatch stochastic gradient descent is used to conduct training. This work is motivated by our observation that NWP models trained under FL exhibited remarkably less propensity to such memorization compared to the central learning setting. Thus, we initiate a formal study to understand the effect of different components of FL on unintended memorization in trained NWP models. Our results show that several differing components of FL play an important role in reducing unintended memorization. First, we discover that the clustering of data according to users—which happens by design in FL—has the most significant effect in reducing such memorization. Using the Federated Averaging optimizer with larger effective minibatch sizes for training causes a further reduction. We also demonstrate that training in FL with a user-level differential privacy guarantee results in models that can provide high utility while being resilient to memorizing *out-of-distribution* phrases with thousands of insertions across over a hundred users in the training set.

1 Introduction

There is a growing line of work (Fredrikson et al., 2015; Wu et al., 2016; Shokri et al., 2017; Carlini et al., 2018; Song and Shmatikov, 2019) demonstrating that neural networks can leak information about the underlying training data in unexpected ways. Many of these works show that language models (LMs), which include commonly-used next word prediction (NWP) models, are prone to *unintentionally memorize* rarely-occurring phrases in the data. Large-scale LM training often involves training over sensitive data, and such memorization can result in blatant leaks of privacy (e.g., (Munroe, 2019)). Thus, it is crucial to measure such memorization in trained LMs, and identify mitigation techniques to ensure privacy of the training data.

The framework of Federated Learning (FL) (McMahan et al., 2017a; McMahan and Ramage, 2017) has emerged as a popular approach for training neural networks on a large corpus of decentralized on-device data (e.g., (Konečný et al., 2016; Konecný et al., 2016; Bonawitz et al., 2017; Hard et al., 2018; Bonawitz et al., 2019)). FL operates in an iterative fashion: in each round, sampled client devices receive the current global model from a central server to compute an update on their locally-stored data, and the server aggregates these updates using, for e.g., the Federated Averaging (FedAvg) algorithm (McMahan et al., 2017a), to build a new global model. A hallmark of FL is that each participating device only sends model weights to the central server; raw data never leaves the device, remaining locally-cached. This, by itself, is not sufficient to provide formal privacy guarantees for the training data. However, this work is motivated by the observation (described in detail in Section 3) that NWP models trained under the canonical setting of FL exhibited resilience to memorize rare phrases in spite of hundreds of occurrences in the training data. Note that FL does differ in many aspects from the well-studied (Shokri et al., 2017; Carlini et al., 2018; Song and Shmatikov, 2019) *central learning* setting where all the data is stored at a central server, and minibatch stochastic gradient descent (SGD) is used to conduct training. While training NWP models via central learning, we observed that phrases with even tens of occurrences were easily

Proceedings of the 58th Annual Meeting of the Association for Computational Linguistics, pages 1–10
July 5–10, 2020.
https://doi.org/10.26615/978-954-452-056-4_001

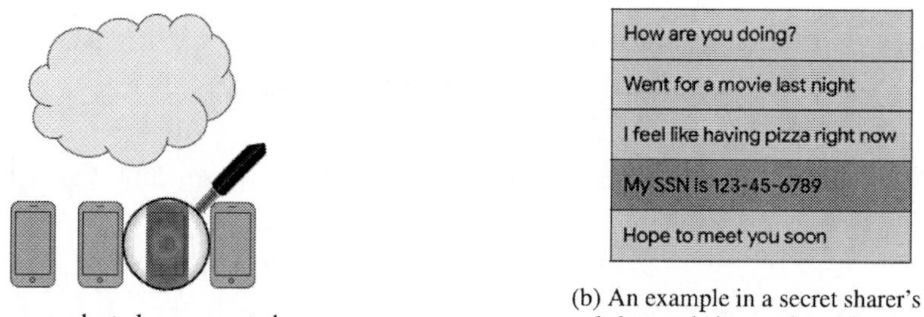

(a) A user selected as a secret sharer for a canary.

(b) An example in a secret sharer's local dataset being replaced by the canary.

Figure 1: An illustration of our federated secret-sharer framework, using the canary "My SSN is 123-45-6789".

memorized, in line with prior work (Carlini et al., 2018) that showed the propensity of such models to memorize phrases with even one occurrence in the training set. Thus, we initiate a formal study to understand the effect of the different components of FL, compared to the central learning setting, on unintended memorization in trained NWP models.

We also study the extent to which a guarantee of Differential Privacy (DP) (Dwork et al., 2006c,a) reduces such memorization. DP has become the standard for performing learning tasks over sensitive data, and has been adopted by companies like Google (Erlingsson et al., 2014; Bittau et al., 2017; Erlingsson et al., 2020), Apple (Apple, 2017), Microsoft (Ding et al., 2017), and LinkedIn (Rogers et al., 2020), as well as the US Census Bureau (Kuo et al., 2018). Intuitively, DP prevents an adversary from confidently making conclusions about whether any particular user's data was used to train a model, even while having access to the model and arbitrary external side information.

The Federated Secret Sharer: We build on the "secret sharer" framework (Carlini et al., 2018) that was designed to measure the unintended memorization in generative models. At a high-level, *out-of-distribution* examples (called canaries) are inserted into a training corpus, and a model trained on this corpus is then evaluated using various techniques to measure the extent to which the model has *memorized* the canaries. Since datasets in FL are inherently partitioned according to users, we adapt the secret sharer framework to the FL regime by introducing two parameters to control the presence of a canary in such settings. An illustration of our federated secret sharer framework is shown in Figure 1. Given a canary with parameters p_u and p_e, we let p_u be the probability with which each user in a dataset is selected to be a "secret sharer" of the canary (Figure 1a), whereas p_e denotes the probability with which each example in such a secret sharer's data is replaced by the canary (Figure 1b). We use Poisson sampling for both user-selection and example-replacement. The secret sharer selection phase precedes canary insertion to model real-world settings where occurrences of user-specific unique or rare out-of-distribution canaries are typically limited to a small group of users, but such users can exhibit high usage for those canaries.

Contributions: Our empirical evaluations demonstrate the following key contributions. First, we observe that clustering training data according to users, which happens by design in distributed learning settings like FL, has a significant effect in reducing unintended memorization for NWP models. Next, given a dataset partitioned by users, we show that replacing the learning optimizer from SGD to Federated Averaging and increasing the effective minibatch size provides a further reduction in such memorization. Lastly, we demonstrate that training in FL with *user-level* differential privacy (DP) results in models that can provide comparable utility while being resilient to memorizing canaries with thousands of insertions spread across over a hundred users in the training set. Prior work (Carlini et al., 2018) has shown that models trained with *record-level* DP do not exhibit unintended memorization for a single insertion of a canary. We provide evidence of models being resilient to memorizing canaries for orders of magnitude higher insertions, at the stronger user-level privacy.

1.1 Related Work

Apart from (Carlini et al., 2018) which this work builds upon, other works (Song and Shmatikov, 2019) have also studied memorization in generative text models. The FL paradigm, which is a major focus of this work, has been used to train multiple production scale models (Hard et al., 2018; Ramaswamy et al., 2019; Chen et al.). Kairouz et al. (2019) provides an excellent overview of the state-of-the-art in the field, along with a suite of interesting open problems. This work also studies the effectiveness of a user-level DP guarantee in reducing unintended memorization. While many works on DP focus on *record-level* DP guarantees (which usually cannot be directly extended to strong user-level DP guarantees), recent works (e.g., (McMahan et al., 2017b; Jain et al., 2018; Augenstein et al., 2020; Andrew et al., 2021)) have designed techniques tailored to user-level DP guarantees.

2 Contrasting Federated Learning with Central Learning

Now, we take a deeper look at how the well-studied central learning framework differs from the canonical setting of FL for LM training. We are interested in differences that might have an effect on unintended memorization. We identify three such components: (1) *Data Processed per Update:* Central learning typically ingests data as *records*/sentences. On the other hand, FL operates at the granularity of a *user*, with each user having their own set of sentences locally. Typically, the amount of data processed per model update in central learning is much smaller in comparison to FL. (2) *Learning Technique:* In central learning, the model is updated via SGD on a minibatch of records. In the canonical setting of FL, a model update typically corresponds to Federated Averaging over a minibatch of users: an average of the differences between the current model and the model obtained after several SGD steps on the local data of a user. (3) *Independent and Identically Distributed (IID) Data:* To reduce variance in learning, the data in central learning is shuffled before training (and/or each update involves a randomly sampled minibatch). Thus, each minibatch can be estimated to be drawn IID from the data. Datasets in FL are naturally grouped according to potentially heterogeneous users, resulting in non-IID data even though each minibatch of users may be randomly sampled.[1]

[1]We do not discuss unbalanced datasets, i.e., the fact that users can have varying amounts of local data, since Federated Averaging in FL deals with such imbalances by weighing each client update according to the size of its local data.

3 Empirical Evaluation

Experimental Setup: Our model architecture (1.3M parameters) mirrors the one used in Hard et al. (2018). We create a modified version of the Stack Overflow dataset (Overflow, 2018) hosted by TensorFlow Federated (Ingerman and Ostrowski, 2019), containing 392K users (93M records). For an IID version of this dataset, we randomly shuffle all the records, and create *synthetic* users having data assigned sequentially from the shuffled records. Since our model is a word-level language model, we follow the methodology used by Carlini et al. (2018) for their experiments with the GMail Smart Compose model (Chen et al., 2019). We insert random 5-word canaries with configurations in the cross product of $p_u \in \{1/50\text{K}, 3/50\text{K}, 1/5\text{K}\}$ and $p_e \in \{1\%, 10\%, 100\%\}$, with 10 different canaries for each (p_u, p_e) configuration, resulting in the insertion of 90 different canaries. Given a prefix of a canary, we use two methods to evaluate the unintended memorization of the suffix for a model: Random Sampling (RS), which for a 2-word prefix measures if the canary has the least log-perplexity among 2M random suffixes, and Beam Search (BS), which uses a greedy beam search to see if the canary is in its top 5 most-likely 5-word continuations from a 1-word prefix. We measure the utility of a model with accuracy and perplexity on the test partition of the unmodified Stack Overflow dataset.

Empirical Results: We present the results of our experiments on evaluating unintended memorization under different training regimes ranging from canonical FL to central learning. For all our experiments using SGD, we train models for 37.5M steps, whereas we train for 8000 rounds for the experiments using FedAvg. For the largest minibatch sizes used in both settings (256 records for SGD, and 5000 users for FedAvg), these checkpoints correspond to training for 100 epochs. Table 1 shows the number of canaries (out of 90) that show up as memorized via both the RS and BS methods. The utility of all the evaluated models is similar; accuracy varies from $23.7 - 24.6\%$, and perplexity varies from $57.3 - 64.3$ across all models.[2]

Training in FL with DP Federated Averaging (DP-FedAvg): Next, we evaluate the extent to which training using DP-FedAvg is resilient to such

[2]We defer the utility measurements to Table 3.

Optimizer	Data	Batch Size	RS	BS
FedAvg	Non-IID	500 users	21	0
		1K users	23	1
		2K users	19	1
		5K users	26	2
	IID	500 users	66	56
		1K users	69	58
		2K users	67	56
		5K users	65	58
SGD	Non-IID	32 records	37	19
		64 records	49	36
		128 records	48	34
		256 records	51	39
	IID	32 records	54	42
		64 records	54	42
		128 records	52	45
		256 records	53	43

Table 1: Results for the number of inserted canaries (out of 90) memorized via the Random Sampling (RS) and Beam Search (BS) methods for various models evaluated at 8000 rounds when sampling users (FedAvg), and 37.5M steps when sampling records (SGD).

memorization. To provide the strongest user-level DP while obtaining high utility, we conduct experiments only for our largest minibatch size of 5K users. The results are presented in Table 2.

Optimizer	RS	BS	Acc. %	Perp.
FedAvg	26	2	24.5	58.2
DP-FedAvg	12	0	23.3	68.5

Table 2: Unintended memorization and utility for a model trained with $(18.8, 10^{-7})$-DP in FL (non-IID users) with 5k users/round for 100 epochs.

3.1 Discussion

Clustering data according to users: The results from our experiments strongly indicate that clustering data according to users significantly reduces unintended memorization. This is evident by considering the measurements in Table 1 in pairs where the only differing component among them is whether the data is IID or not. The number of epochs taken over the dataset to train the models on which we measure memorization is the same for any particular minibatch size, irrespective of whether the data is IID. Thus, the number of times the inserted canaries were encountered during training is the same. However, the amount of memorization observed is always lower when the data is Non-IID. This effect is more pronounced in the settings where FedAvg is used as the training method. For instance, for a minibatch size of $b_u = 500$ users, training with FedAvg on IID data results in 66 (56) canaries showing up as memorized via the RS (BS) method. The same configuration on Non-IID data results in the RS method classifying only 21 canaries as memorized, and the BS method not being able to extract any canary even after 8000 rounds of training. In addition to the data being clustered, the inserted canaries are clustered as well, which we conjecture to be playing a crucial role in reducing such memorization.

Varying data per update: Fixing the optimizer to SGD/FedAvg and the data to be IID/non-IID, we do not see any significant effect of varying the minibatch size on such memorization.[3]

Training non-IID user data with FedAvg and larger effective minibatches: The smallest minibatch size for our FedAvg experiments is 500 users,[4] and as each user contains ≈ 250 records, the *effective* minibatch size is ≈ 125K records. In comparison, the largest minibatch size for which we are able to conduct SGD training is 256 records. Focusing on the results in Table 1 using Non-IID data, we find that using FedAvg and having larger effective minibatches per round causes a significant reduction in unintended memorization when compared to training with SGD and smaller minibatches.[5]

Training with DP-FedAvg in FL: Our aim is to test the extent to which NWP models trained with DP-FedAvg in FL are resilient to such memorization. By definition, a user-level DP guarantee is intended to be resilient to changes w.r.t. any one

[3]For the case of SGD and Non-IID data, while unintended memorization does seem to increase with the minibatch size, we do not observe the increase consistently. Additional investigation for potential causes of such a trend are beyond the scope of this work.

[4]We do not train with smaller user minibatch sizes as we want the number of training epochs for the lowest settings in FedAvg and SGD to be similar at 8000 training rounds.

[5]Looking at the same set of results for IID data, the trend seems to be moving in the direction of increasing memorization. However, since the magnitude of the effect is much smaller, we deem that further investigation is required for this case, which we leave for future work.

user's data. Some of our inserted canaries are shared by $\sim$100 users (with $\sim$24.5K occurrences in the training data). In spite of such high levels of canary insertion, and our FL models exhibiting the least amount of unintended memorization (Table 1), we see that training with DP-FedAvg results in a significantly reduced memorization. Our results are noteworthy as, in spite of our DP model exhibiting extremely low unintended memorization, it also provides comparable utility as a model trained via FedAvg, along with a user-level guarantee of $(18.8, 10^{-7})$-DP. While strengthening the privacy guarantee of DP-FedAvg by increasing the noise added to the model update in each training round can further reduce such memorization, it can also start significantly affecting model utility. Designing methods that improve the privacy-utility trade-offs is an interesting direction, which is beyond the scope of this work.

4 Conclusion

In this work, we conduct a formal study to understand the effect of the different components of Federated Learning (FL), on the unintended memorization in trained next word prediction (NWP) models, as compared to the well-studied central learning. From our results, we observe that the components of FL exhibit a synergy in reducing such memorization. To our surprise, user-based clustering of data (which occurs as a natural consequence in the FL setting) has the most significant effect in the reduction. Moreover, training using Federated Averaging and larger effective minibatches reduces such memorization further. Lastly, we observe that training in FL with a user-level differential privacy guarantee results in models that can provide comparable utility while being resilient to memorizing canaries with thousands of insertions across over a hundred users in the training set.

Recent work (Karimireddy et al., 2019) has shown that, in general, such heterogeneity in the training data can result in a slower and unstable convergence due to factors such as "client-drift". For all of the experiments with non-IID data, we observe that the utility of the trained models is comparable to those trained on IID data, and we leave further exploration into why client-drift may not play a significant role in our experiments for future work. Next, while our extensive evaluation is for a practical NWP model on a real-world benchmark dataset, the degree of unintended memorization in general can depend on the model architecture and the dataset used for training. Lastly, the secret-sharer line of methods for measuring unintended memorization operate at the granularity of a record. For future work, it will be interesting to design stronger attacks targeting data at the granularity of a user, and measure the resilience of models trained via FL, against such memorization.

Acknowledgements

The authors would like to thank Mingqing Chen, Andrew Hard, and Gautam Kamath for their helpful comments towards improving the paper.

References

Galen Andrew, Om Thakkar, H. Brendan McMahan, and Swaroop Ramaswamy. 2021. Differentially private learning with adaptive clipping.

Differential Privacy Team Apple. 2017. Learning with privacy at scale.

Sean Augenstein, H. Brendan McMahan, Daniel Ramage, Swaroop Ramaswamy, Peter Kairouz, Mingqing Chen, Rajiv Mathews, and Blaise Agüera y Arcas. 2020. Generative models for effective ML on private, decentralized datasets. In *8th International Conference on Learning Representations, ICLR 2020, Addis Ababa, Ethiopia, April 26-30, 2020*. OpenReview.net.

Andrea Bittau, Úlfar Erlingsson, Petros Maniatis, Ilya Mironov, Ananth Raghunathan, David Lie, Mitch Rudominer, Ushasree Kode, Julien Tinnés, and Bernhard Seefeld. 2017. Prochlo: Strong privacy for analytics in the crowd. In *Proceedings of the 26th Symposium on Operating Systems Principles, Shanghai, China, October 28-31, 2017*, pages 441–459. ACM.

Keith Bonawitz, Hubert Eichner, Wolfgang Grieskamp, Dzmitry Huba, Alex Ingerman, Vladimir Ivanov, Chloé Kiddon, Jakub Konecný, Stefano Mazzocchi, H. Brendan McMahan, Timon Van Overveldt, David Petrou, Daniel Ramage, and Jason Roselander. 2019. Towards federated learning at scale: System design. *CoRR*, abs/1902.01046.

Keith Bonawitz, Vladimir Ivanov, Ben Kreuter, Antonio Marcedone, H. Brendan McMahan, Sarvar Patel, Daniel Ramage, Aaron Segal, and Karn Seth. 2017. Practical secure aggregation for privacy-preserving machine learning. In *Proceedings of the 2017 Association for Computing Machinery (ACM) Special Interest Group on Security, Audit and Control (SIGSAC) Conference on Computer and Communications Security*, CCS '17, pages 1175–1191, New York, NY, USA. ACM.

Nicholas Carlini, Chang Liu, Jernej Kos, Úlfar Erlingsson, and Dawn Song. 2018. The secret sharer: Measuring unintended neural network memorization & extracting secrets. *Computing Research Repository (CoRR)*, abs/1802.08232.

Mia Xu Chen, Benjamin N Lee, Gagan Bansal, Yuan Cao, Shuyuan Zhang, Justin Lu, Jackie Tsay, Yinan Wang, Andrew M Dai, Zhifeng Chen, et al. 2019. Gmail smart compose: Real-time assisted writing. In *Proceedings of the 25th ACM SIGKDD International Conference on Knowledge Discovery & Data Mining*, pages 2287–2295.

Mingqing Chen, Ananda Theertha Suresh, Rajiv Mathews, Adeline Wong, Cyril Allauzen, Françoise Beaufays, and Michael Riley. Federated learning of n-gram language models. In *Proceedings of the 23rd Conference on Computational Natural Language Learning, CoNLL 2019, Hong Kong, China, November 3-4, 2019*.

Bolin Ding, Janardhan Kulkarni, and Sergey Yekhanin. 2017. Collecting telemetry data privately. In *Advances in Neural Information Processing Systems 30: Annual Conference on Neural Information Processing Systems 2017, 4-9 December 2017, Long Beach, CA, USA*, pages 3571–3580.

Cynthia Dwork, Krishnaram Kenthapadi, Frank McSherry, Ilya Mironov, and Moni Naor. 2006a. Our data, ourselves: Privacy via distributed noise generation. In *EUROCRYPT*, pages 486–503.

Cynthia Dwork, Krishnaram Kenthapadi, Frank Mcsherry, Ilya Mironov, and Moni Naor. 2006b. Our data, ourselves: Privacy via distributed noise generation. In *EUROCRYPT*, pages 486–503.

Cynthia Dwork, Frank McSherry, Kobbi Nissim, and Adam Smith. 2006c. Calibrating noise to sensitivity in private data analysis. In *Theory of Cryptography Conference*, pages 265–284. Springer.

Úlfar Erlingsson, Vitaly Feldman, Ilya Mironov, Ananth Raghunathan, Shuang Song, Kunal Talwar, and Abhradeep Thakurta. 2020. Encode, shuffle, analyze privacy revisited: Formalizations and empirical evaluation. *CoRR*, abs/2001.03618.

Úlfar Erlingsson, Vasyl Pihur, and Aleksandra Korolova. 2014. Rappor: Randomized aggregatable privacy-preserving ordinal response. In *Proceedings of the 2014 Association for Computing Machinery (ACM) SIGSAC conference on computer and communications security*, pages 1054–1067. Association for Computing Machinery (ACM).

Matt Fredrikson, Somesh Jha, and Thomas Ristenpart. 2015. Model inversion attacks that exploit confidence information and basic countermeasures. In *Proceedings of the 22Nd Association for Computing Machinery (ACM) SIGSAC Conference on Computer and Communications Security*, CCS '15, pages 1322–1333, New York, NY, USA. Association for Computing Machinery (ACM).

Andrew Hard, Kanishka Rao, Rajiv Mathews, Françoise Beaufays, Sean Augenstein, Hubert Eichner, Chloé Kiddon, and Daniel Ramage. 2018. Federated learning for mobile keyboard prediction. *CoRR*, abs/1811.03604.

Alex Ingerman and Krzys Ostrowski. 2019. Introducing tensorflow federated.

Prateek Jain, Om Thakkar, and Abhradeep Thakurta. 2018. Differentially private matrix completion revisited. In *Proceedings of the 35th International Conference on Machine Learning, ICML 2018, Stockholmsmässan, Stockholm, Sweden, July 10-15, 2018*, pages 2220–2229.

Peter Kairouz, H. Brendan McMahan, Brendan Avent, Aurélien Bellet, Mehdi Bennis, Arjun Nitin Bhagoji, Keith Bonawitz, Zachary Charles, Graham Cormode, Rachel Cummings, Rafael G. L. D'Oliveira, Salim El Rouayheb, David Evans, Josh Gardner, Zachary Garrett, Adrià Gascón, Badih Ghazi, Phillip B. Gibbons, Marco Gruteser, Zaïd Harchaoui, Chaoyang He, Lie He, Zhouyuan Huo, Ben Hutchinson, Justin Hsu, Martin Jaggi, Tara Javidi, Gauri Joshi, Mikhail Khodak, Jakub Konecný, Aleksandra Korolova, Farinaz Koushanfar, Sanmi Koyejo, Tancrède Lepoint, Yang Liu, Prateek Mittal, Mehryar Mohri, Richard Nock, Ayfer Özgür, Rasmus Pagh, Mariana Raykova, Hang Qi, Daniel Ramage, Ramesh Raskar, Dawn Song, Weikang Song, Sebastian U. Stich, Ziteng Sun, Ananda Theertha Suresh, Florian Tramèr, Praneeth Vepakomma, Jianyu Wang, Li Xiong, Zheng Xu, Qiang Yang, Felix X. Yu, Han Yu, and Sen Zhao. 2019. Advances and open problems in federated learning. *CoRR*, abs/1912.04977.

Sai Praneeth Karimireddy, Satyen Kale, Mehryar Mohri, Sashank J. Reddi, Sebastian U. Stich, and Ananda Theertha Suresh. 2019. SCAFFOLD: stochastic controlled averaging for on-device federated learning. *CoRR*, abs/1910.06378.

Diederik P. Kingma and Jimmy Ba. 2015. Adam: A method for stochastic optimization. In *3rd International Conference on Learning Representations, ICLR 2015, San Diego, CA, USA, May 7-9, 2015, Conference Track Proceedings*.

Jakub Konecný, H. Brendan McMahan, Felix X. Yu, Peter Richtárik, Ananda Theertha Suresh, and Dave Bacon. 2016. Federated learning: Strategies for improving communication efficiency. *Computing Research Repository (CoRR)*, abs/1610.05492.

Jakub Konečný, H. Brendan McMahan, Daniel Ramage, and Peter Richtárik. 2016. Federated optimization: Distributed machine learning for on-device intelligence. *ArXiv*, abs/1610.02527.

Yu-Hsuan Kuo, Cho-Chun Chiu, Daniel Kifer, Michael Hay, and Ashwin Machanavajjhala. 2018. Differentially private hierarchical count-of-counts histograms. *PVLDB*, 11(11):1509–1521.

Brendan McMahan, Eider Moore, Daniel Ramage, Seth Hampson, and Blaise Agüera y Arcas. 2017a. Communication-efficient learning of deep networks from decentralized data. In *Proceedings of the 20th International Conference on Artificial Intelligence and Statistics, AISTATS 2017, 20-22 April 2017, Fort Lauderdale, FL, USA*, pages 1273–1282.

Brendan McMahan and Daniel Ramage. 2017. Federated learning: Collaborative machine learning without centralized training data. *Google Research Blog*, 3.

H. Brendan McMahan, Daniel Ramage, Kunal Talwar, and Li Zhang. 2017b. Learning differentially private language models without losing accuracy. *CoRR*, abs/1710.06963.

I. Mironov. 2017. Rényi differential privacy. In *2017 Institute of Electrical and Electronics Engineers (IEEE) 30th Computer Security Foundations Symposium (CSF)*, pages 263–275.

Randall Munroe. 2019. xkcd: Predictive models. `https://xkcd.com/2169/`.

Stack Overflow. 2018. The Stack Overflow Data. `https://www.kaggle.com/stackoverflow/stackoverflow`.

Ning Qian. 1999. On the momentum term in gradient descent learning algorithms. *Neural Networks*, 12(1):145–151.

Swaroop Ramaswamy, Rajiv Mathews, Kanishka Rao, and Françoise Beaufays. 2019. Federated learning for emoji prediction in a mobile keyboard.

Ryan Rogers, Subbu Subramaniam, Sean Peng, David Durfee, Seunghyun Lee, Santosh Kumar Kancha, Shraddha Sahay, and Parvez Ahammad. 2020. Linkedin's audience engagements api: A privacy preserving data analytics system at scale.

R. Shokri, M. Stronati, C. Song, and V. Shmatikov. 2017. Membership inference attacks against machine learning models. In *2017 Institute of Electrical and Electronics Engineers (IEEE) Symposium on Security and Privacy (SP)*, pages 3–18.

Congzheng Song and Vitaly Shmatikov. 2019. Auditing data provenance in text-generation models. In *Proceedings of the 25th ACM SIGKDD International Conference on Knowledge Discovery & Data Mining, KDD 2019, Anchorage, AK, USA, August 4-8, 2019*, pages 196–206. ACM.

Yu-Xiang Wang, Borja Balle, and Shiva Prasad Kasiviswanathan. 2019. Subsampled renyi differential privacy and analytical moments accountant. In *The 22nd International Conference on Artificial Intelligence and Statistics, AISTATS 2019, 16-18 April 2019, Naha, Okinawa, Japan*, pages 1226–1235.

X. Wu, M. Fredrikson, S. Jha, and J. F. Naughton. 2016. A methodology for formalizing model-inversion attacks. In *2016 Institute of Electrical and Electronics Engineers (IEEE) 29th Computer Security Foundations Symposium (CSF)*, pages 355–370.

A Preliminaries

A.1 Measuring Unintended Memorization

Following (Carlini et al., 2018), this work assumes a threat model of curious or malevolent users having a black-box query access to models, in that they see only the models' output probabilities (or logits). We also assume that users can adaptively query models multiple times, thus posing a threat of extracting uncommon word combinations.

Now, we describe the Secret Sharer framework of (Carlini et al., 2018). First, random sequences called canaries are inserted into the training data. The canaries are constructed based on a prefixed format sequence. For instance, to design the framework for a character-level model, the format could be "My SSN is xxx-xx-$xxxx$", where each x can take a random value from digits 0 to 9. Next, the target model is trained on the modified dataset containing the canaries. Lastly, methods like Random Sampling and Beam Search (both formally defined in Section 3) are used to efficiently measure the extent to which the model has "memorized" the inserted random canaries, and whether it is possible for an adversary with partial knowledge to extract the canary. For instance, if a canary is classified as memorized via our Beam Search method, then given black-box access to the trained model, an adversary with the knowledge of only the first word of the inserted canary can extract it completely with a simple beam search.

A.2 Differential Privacy

To establish the notion of differential privacy (Dwork et al., 2006c,b), we first define neighboring datasets. We will refer to a pair of datasets D, D' as neighbors if D' can be obtained by the addition or removal of all the examples associated with one user from D, to be able to provide a user-level DP guarantee.[6]

Definition A.1 (Differential privacy (Dwork et al., 2006c,b)). *A randomized algorithm $\mathcal{A}$ is (ϵ, δ)-differentially private if, for any pair of neighboring*

[6]This is in contrast to a record-level DP guarantee, where neighboring datasets differ in the addition/removal of exactly one example.

datasets D and D', and for all events $\mathcal{S}$ in the output range of $\mathcal{A}$, we have

$$\Pr[\mathcal{A}(D) \in \mathcal{S}] \leq e^{\epsilon} \cdot \Pr[\mathcal{A}(D') \in \mathcal{S}] + \delta$$

where the probability is taken over the random coins of $\mathcal{A}$.

For meaningful privacy guarantees, ϵ is assumed to be a small constant, and $\delta \ll 1/|D|$.

To train models with DP guarantees, we follow the variant of DP Federated Averaging (DP-FedAvg) (McMahan et al., 2017b) used in (Augenstein et al., 2020), where the only change is sampling fixed-sized minibatches in each training round.[7]

A.3 Differentially Private Federated Averaging

We now present the technique used to train our DP model in FL. It closely follows the DP-FedAvg technique in (McMahan et al., 2017b), in that per-user updates are clipped to have a bounded L_2 norm, and calibrated Gaussian noise is added to the weighted average update to be used for computing the model to be sent in the next round. A slight difference between the DP-FedAvg algorithm in (McMahan et al., 2017b) and our approach is the way in which client devices are sampled to participate in a given federated round of computation. DP-FedAvg uses Poisson sampling, where for each round, each user is selected independently with a fixed probability. In this work (also, following (Augenstein et al., 2020)), we instead use fixed-size federated rounds, where a fixed number of users is randomly sampled to participate in each round. For reference, we provide a pseudo-code for the technique in Algorithm 1.

Privacy analysis: Following the analysis of this technique in (Augenstein et al., 2020), we obtain our DP guarantees by using the following:

1. the analytical moments accountant (Wang et al., 2019) to obtain the Rényi differential privacy (RDP) guarantee for a federated round of computation that is based on the subsampled Gaussian mechanism,

2. Proposition 1 (Mironov, 2017) for computing the RDP guarantee of the composition involving all the rounds, and

[7]Due to a technical limitation of the simulation framework, our experiments use sampling with replacement instead of without replacement; this should have negligible impact on the metrics of the trained models.

Main training loop:
parameters: round participation fraction $q \in (0, 1]$, total user population $N \in \mathbb{N}$, noise scale $z \in \mathcal{R}^+$, clip parameter $S \in \mathcal{R}^+$

Initialize model θ^0, moments accountant $\mathcal{M}$
Set $\sigma = \frac{zS}{qW}$
for each round $t = 0, 1, 2, \ldots$ **do**
  $\mathcal{C}^t \leftarrow$ (sample without replacement qN users from population)
  for each user $k \in \mathcal{C}^t$ **in parallel do**
    $\Delta_k^{t+1} \leftarrow \text{UserUpdate}(k, \theta^t)$
  $\Delta^{t+1} = \frac{1}{qN} \sum_{k \in \mathcal{C}^t} \Delta_k^{t+1}$
  $\theta^{t+1} \leftarrow \theta^t + \Delta^{t+1} + \mathcal{N}(0, I\sigma^2)$
  $\mathcal{M}$.accum_priv_spending(z)
print $\mathcal{M}$.get_privacy_spent()

UserUpdate(k, θ^0):
parameters: number of local epochs $E \in \mathbb{N}$, batch size $B \in \mathbb{N}$, learning rate $\eta \in \mathcal{R}^+$, clip parameter $S \in \mathcal{R}^+$, loss function $\ell(\theta; b)$

$\theta \leftarrow \theta^0$
for each local epoch i from 1 to E **do**
  $\mathcal{B} \leftarrow$ (k's data split into size B batches)
  for each batch $b \in \mathcal{B}$ **do**
    $\theta \leftarrow \theta - \eta \nabla \ell(\theta; b)$
$\Delta = \theta - \theta^0$
return update $\Delta_k = \Delta \cdot \min\left(1, \frac{S}{\|\Delta\|}\right)$ *// Clip*

Algorithm 1: Differentially Private Federated Averaging (DP-FedAvg) with fixed-size federated rounds, used to train our DP NWP model.

3. Proposition 3 (Mironov, 2017) to obtain a DP guarantee from the composed RDP guarantee.

B Additional Empirical Evaluation

In this section, we present the results of our additional empirical evaluation that was omitted from the main body.

Utility Metrics: Here, we present the utility metrics for all the models for which the unintended memorization results were presented in Table 1. It is easy to see that the utility of all the evaluated models is similar; the accuracy varies from $23.7 - 24.6\%$, and the perplexity varies from $57.3 - 64.3$ across all the models.

Using Different Optimizers: In Table 4, we provide the results for using different optimizers like Momentum (Qian, 1999) and Adam (Kingma and Ba, 2015) for training. We conduct experiments using only the smallest batch size in both the granularities (32 records, or 500 users). For Momentum, we set the momentum parameter to 0.9, and for

Optimizer	Data	Batch size	Acc.	Perp.
FedAvg	Non-IID	500 users	24.4	58.8
		1K users	24.3	59.5
		2K users	24.5	58.3
		5K users	24.5	58.2
	IID	500 users	24.6	57.5
		1K users	24.6	57.3
		2K users	24.6	57.4
		5K users	24.6	57.3
SGD	Non-IID	32 records	23.7	64.3
		64 records	24.1	61.8
		128 records	24.1	61.5
		256 records	24.1	61.3
	IID	32 records	24	62.2
		64 records	24.1	61.5
		128 records	24	62
		256 records	24.1	61.1

Table 3: Results for the utility metrics for various models evaluated at 8000 rounds when sampling users (FedAvg), and 37.5M steps when sampling records (SGD). Acc. denotes test accuracy (in %), and Perp. denotes test perplexity.

Data	Batch Size	Opt.	RS, BS	Acc. (%), Perp.
IID	32 rec.	SGD	54, 42	24, 62.2
		Mom.	64, 50	24.2, 60.6
		Adam	56, 42	22.7, 70.8
	500 users	FedAvg	66, 56	24.6, 57.5
		FedAvg + Adam	60, 46	23.7, 63.7
Non-IID	32 rec.	SGD	37, 19	23.7, 64.3
		Mom.	48, 36	24.3, 59.9
		Adam	21, 13	21.5, 84.1
	500 users	FedAvg	21, 0	24.4, 58.8
		FedAvg + Adam	8, 0	23.3, 66.5

Table 4: Unintended memorization, and utility metrics for models using different optimizers evaluated at 37.5M steps when sampling records (e.g., SGD), and 8000 rounds when sampling users (e.g., FedAvg). Mom. denotes the Momentum optimizer.

Optimizer	RS	BS	Acc. %	Perp.
FedAvg	65	58	24.6	57.3
DP-FedAvg	48	42	23.9	63

Table 5: Unintended memorization and utility for models trained with $(18.8, 10^{-7})$-DP using DP-FedAvg on IID data and 5K users/round for 100 epochs.

Adam, we set the learning rate to 10^{-4}. First, we observe that using Momentum increases the observed unintended memorization but has a similar utility as SGD. On the other hand, we see that using Adam decreases such memorization, but the utility of the models is also noticeably reduced as compared to SGD. We observe a similar trend when Adam is combined with FedAvg.

Training with DP-FedAvg on IID data: Now, we present in Table 5 the results of using DP-FedAvg as the optimizer on IID data consisting of synthetic users. We observe that using DP-FedAvg provides a significant reduction in unintended memorization compared to using FedAvg.

Only Clipping: To bound the contribution by each participating user, DP-FedAvg clips each user update before aggregating them from a minibatch of users and adding calibrated noise to guarantee DP. Following (Carlini et al., 2018), we present results (rows containing "FedAvg+Clip" in Table 6) for the case when user updates are clipped to a value of 0.2, but no noise is added. This results in an (∞, δ)-DP guarantee for any $\delta \in (0, 1)$, which is vacuous as a privacy guarantee. However, this experiment helps us observe the extent to which only clipping reduces the propensity of unintended memorization exhibited by trained models. With IID data, for the setting evaluated in Section 3 (8000 rounds, i.e., 100 epochs for minibatch size of 5000 users), we observe that the RS method extracts 58 canaries with clipping, which is 7 fewer canaries when compared to without clipping. The BS method extracts 49, which is 9 fewer than without clipping. For Non-IID data, we observe a similar trend but it is more pronounced: the RS method extracts 11 canaries with clipping, which is 15 fewer canaries when compared to without clipping, whereas the BS method is not able to extract any of the inserted canaries.

Evaluating for Same Training Epochs: In Table 7, we provide the results for evaluating models trained for the same number of epochs over the training data. For the runs using SGD, we start

Data	Optimizer	RS, BS	Acc. (%), Perp.
IID	FedAvg	65, 58	24.6, 57.3
	FedAvg+Clip	58, 49	24.2, 60
Non-IID	FedAvg	26, 2	24.5, 58.2
	FedAvg+Clip	11, 0	24, 61.5

Table 6: Unintended memorization, lowest (by insertion frequency) canary configuration memorized, and utility for models trained with Clipping/DP and 5000 users/round for 100 epochs. The models trained with DP-FedAvg satisfy $(18.8, 10^{-7})$-DP.

with a batch size of 32 records and a tuned learning rate of 0.005, and we increase the learning rate by $\approx \sqrt{2}$ for every 2x increase in the batch size. For all the experiments with FedAvg, we find that using a constant learning rate provides the best utility across the different batch sizes, and thus, we keep it fixed.

Opt.	Data	Batch Size	RS, BS	Acc. (%), Perp.
SGD	IID	32 rec.	49, 43	23.9, 63
		64 rec.	51, 39	23.5, 65.1
		128 rec.	46, 36	23.2, 67.6
		256 rec.	46, 32	23, 69.7
	Non-IID	32 rec.	40, 29	23.7, 64.2
		64 rec.	38, 32	23.6, 65.6
		128 rec.	35, 26	23.2, 68.2
		256 rec.	40, 31	23, 69.8
Fed-Avg	IID	500 users	66, 56	24.6, 57.5
		1k users	27, 18	24.5, 58
		2k users	28, 18	24.4, 59.3
		5k users	28, 18	24, 62.5
	Non-IID	500 users	21, 0	24.4, 58.8
		1k users	10, 0	24, 61.2
		2k users	0, 0	24, 61.9
		5k users	0, 0	23.3, 67.9

Table 7: Results for the number of inserted canaries (out of 90) memorized via the RS and BS methods, and utility metrics for various models evaluated at $\approx$10 epochs of training.

For the models trained with SGD, for both IID and non-IID data we observe that unintended memorization remains comparable for models trained with different batch sizes. However, we see a decrease in the utility as the batch size increases. The decrease in utility is observed for models trained using FedAvg as well, but we also observe a significant drop in the such memorization when training is performed with at least 1000 users per round. Moreover, once the training involves at least 2000 users on non-IID data, both the RS and BS methods are unsuccessful in classifying any of the 90 inserted canaries as memorized.

On a Utilitarian Approach to Privacy Preserving Text Generation

Zekun Xu
Amazon
Seattle, WA USA
zeku@amazon.com

Abhinav Aggarwal
Amazon
Seattle, WA USA
aggabhin@amazon.com

Oluwaseyi Feyisetan
Amazon
Seattle, WA USA
sey@amazon.com

Nathanael Teissier
Amazon
Arlington, VA USA
natteis@amazon.com

Abstract

Differentially-private mechanisms for text generation typically add carefully calibrated noise to input words and use the nearest neighbor to the noised input as the output word. When the noise is small in magnitude, these mechanisms are susceptible to reconstruction of the original sensitive text. This is because the nearest neighbor to the noised input is likely to be the original input. To mitigate this empirical privacy risk, we propose a novel class of differentially private mechanisms that parameterizes the nearest neighbor selection criterion in traditional mechanisms. Motivated by Vickrey auction, where only the second highest price is revealed and the highest price is kept private, we balance the choice between the first and the second nearest neighbors in the proposed class of mechanisms using a tuning parameter. This parameter is selected by empirically solving a constrained optimization problem for maximizing utility, while maintaining the desired privacy guarantees. We argue that this empirical measurement framework can be used to align different mechanisms along a common benchmark for their privacy-utility tradeoff, particularly when different distance metrics are used to calibrate the amount of noise added. Our experiments on real text classification datasets show up to 50% improvement in utility compared to the existing state-of-the-art with the same empirical privacy guarantee.

1 Introduction

Over the past decade, privacy-preserving machine learning has emerged as a hot topic in a variety of real world speech and language applications. In natural language processing (NLP), ensuring data privacy in machine learning tasks is especially challenging because text data tends to be rich in sensitive and potentially identifiable information about the users that contributed to these datasets.

The literature is replete with approaches proposed for privacy-preserving text analysis, such as replacing sensitive information with general terms (Cumby and Ghani, 2011; Anandan et al., 2012; Sánchez and Batet, 2016), injecting additional words into original texts (Domingo-Ferrer et al., 2009; Pang et al., 2010; Sánchez et al., 2013), as well as k-anonymity and its variants (Sweeney, 2002; Machanavajjhala et al., 2007; Li et al., 2007). However, these methods are provably non-private and have been shown to be vulnerable to re-identification attacks (Korolova et al., 2009; Petit et al., 2015). To ensure a quantifiable privacy guarantee, differential privacy (DP) has become the *de facto* standard for privacy-preserving statistical analysis (Dwork et al., 2006; Dwork, 2008; Dwork et al., 2014), with applications to text analysis.

At a high level, a randomized algorithm is differentially private if the output distributions from any two neighboring databases are (near) indistinguishable. This indistinguishability is controlled by a privacy parameter, which, in the case of text analysis, is often scaled by the distance between neighboring datasets to capture the semantic similarity between different words (Feyisetan et al., 2019; Fernandes et al., 2019; Feyisetan et al., 2020; Xu et al., 2020). This calibration enables the mechanisms to enjoy *metric-DP* (Andrés et al., 2013; Chatzikokolakis et al., 2013), which was first introduced as a generalization of local DP (Kasiviswanathan et al., 2011) for protecting location privacy. Observe that a direct application of local DP mechanisms will be too restrictive because it requires that the probability ratio between the output distributions of any two words in the vocabulary be bounded by some fixed constant. Due to the high dimensional nature of textual tasks and very large vocabulary sizes (e.g. 2.2M words for GLoVe common crawl (Pennington et al., 2014)), this can lead to adding a lot of noise for achieving the desired privacy guarantees, severely impacting the utility of the NLP task.

Comparing Metric-DP Mechanisms. In the context of text analysis, we are given a vocabulary

Proceedings of the 58th Annual Meeting of the Association for Computational Linguistics, pages 11–20
July 5–10, 2020. ©2020 Association for Computational Linguistics
https://doi.org/10.26615/978-954-452-056-4_002

set $\mathcal{W}$ and an embedding function $\phi : \mathcal{W} \to \mathbb{R}^p$, where p is the dimensionality of the embedding model. For any $\epsilon > 0$, a mechanism $M : \mathcal{W} \to \mathcal{W}$ is said to be ϵ differentially private with respect to a given metric $d : \mathbb{R}^p \times \mathbb{R}^p \to [0, \infty)$ if for any $w, w', \hat{w} \in \mathcal{W}$, the following holds:

$$\frac{\Pr\{M(w) = \hat{w}\}}{\Pr\{M(w') = \hat{w}\}} \leq e^{\epsilon d\{\phi(w),\phi(w')\}}. \quad (1)$$

The probabilistic guarantee in (1) ensures that the log probability ratio of observing any output $\hat{w}$ given two inputs w and w' is bounded by $\epsilon d\{\phi(w), \phi(w')\}$. This makes metric-DP less restrictive in that the indistinguishability of the output distributions is scaled by the distance between the inputs. If $d\{\phi(w), \phi(w')\} = \mathbb{1}(w \neq w')$, then metric-DP reduces to standard DP.

Note that while metric-DP allows for a flexible privacy budget calibrated by not only ϵ but also the distance metric, this flexibility makes it harder to interpret the privacy parameter ϵ. For example, in standard DP, $\epsilon = 30$ essentially means negligible privacy guarantee since e^{30} is an astronomically large probability ratio; however, $\epsilon = 30$ is common in the metric-DP literature (Fernandes et al., 2019; Feyisetan et al., 2020; Xu et al., 2020) and still provides meaningful privacy guarantees. This is because the pairwise distance in the word embedding space can be small floating numbers, which brings $\exp(30d\{\phi(w), \phi(w')\})$ to a reasonable scale. Thus, ϵ alone cannot fully characterize the privacy guarantee without the knowledge of the underlying metric space. More importantly, this indicates that the privacy guarantees from DP mechanisms with respect to different metrics are not directly comparable using only their ϵ values.

Our Contributions. A common feature in the existing metric-DP text generation mechanisms is to add a calibrate noise to the input word embedding and then output the nearest neighbor to the noisy embedding as the output. However, when the additive noise is small in magnitude, the input word is likely to remain unchanged, which may constitute an empirical privacy risk because it is trivial for the adversary to reconstruct the original word. To mitigate this issue, we present a novel class of metric-DP text generation mechanisms in this paper. Motivated by the Vickrey auction (Vickrey, 1961) scheme, also known as the second-price auction, we refer to this class of mechanisms as *Vickrey mechanisms*.

Just as in a Vickrey auction, where only the second highest price is revealed[1] and the highest price is kept private, the proposed Vickrey mechanisms generalize the noisy nearest neighbor selection by including the second nearest neighbor in the selection pool using a tuning parameter. The inclusion of the second nearest neighbor greatly reduces the empirical reconstruction risk on the original word.

To select the tuning parameter above, we present a strategy based on optimizing the empirical privacy-utility tradeoff. The empirical privacy measurement is constructed in the context of analysis on de-identified text, which quantifies the risk on how well an adversary can reconstruct the original text based on the observed (possibly perturbed) text. The better the reconstruction, the lower the empirical privacy guarantee. This general framework allows comparing text generation mechanisms that use different distance metrics (see Section 3).

We emphasize that our empirical privacy metric does not supersede the metric-DP guarantee; instead, it provides a new dimension along which different metric-DP mechanisms can be aligned. We say that, within the class of metric-DP mechanisms, an *optimal* mechanism is the one that maximizes the empirical privacy guarantee while keeping the utility loss of the downstream task under some maximum tolerable budget. This definition for privacy-utility tradeoff, modeled as a constrained optimization problem, resembles the literature on protecting privacy for location data (Shokri et al., 2011, 2012; Clark et al., 2019). We extend the analysis for the broader class of metric-DP mechanisms. Additionally, in our experiments, we demonstrate that our proposed Vickrey mechanisms outperform existing mechanisms with respect to the empirical privacy-utility tradeoff on real text classification datasets.

Related Work. Metric-DP (Andrés et al., 2013; Chatzikokolakis et al., 2013; Laud et al., 2020), an extended notion of local DP (Kasiviswanathan et al., 2011), is a popular tool for privacy-preserving text analysis. A text generation mechanism that satisfies DP with respect to the hyperbolic distance metric was proposed in (Feyisetan et al., 2019). This mechanism requires specialized training of word embeddings in the high-dimensional hyperbolic space. For word embeddings in the Euclidean space, like GLOVE (Pennington et al., 2014) or FASTTEXT (Bojanowski et al., 2017), mechanisms like the Laplace mechanism (L_2 met-

[1] to ensure incentive-compatibility

ric) (Fernandes et al., 2019; Feyisetan et al., 2020) and the Mahalanobis mechanism (using a regularized Mahalanobis metric) (Xu et al., 2020) have been proposed. However, a structured comparison of these different mechanisms remains unclear.

Empirical privacy measurements. A variety of empirical techniques for privacy measurement have been proposed for many different applications. In the membership inference attack literature (Shokri et al., 2017; Yeom et al., 2018; Salem et al., 2018; Song and Shmatikov, 2019), an AUC based detectability metric is commonly used to quantify the information leakage from machine learning models about their training data. However, the model trained on a given dataset can only serve as a proxy to estimate its privacy guarantee. Moreover, the detectability metric can vary across different machine learning models and implementations of the inference attack based auditors.

Hypothesis testing based approaches have also been proposed to empirically estimate ϵ (Ding et al., 2018; Gilbert and McMillan, 2018; Liu and Oh, 2019). However, the assumptions in these methods constrain their general applicability. In a recent line of work on privacy-preserving text analysis (Feyisetan et al., 2020; Xu et al., 2020), privacy statistics defined as (i) probability of inputs not being redacted, and (ii) number of distinct outputs given a fixed input, have been used to characterize the empirical privacy of a text generation mechanisms. While those metrics are intuitive and descriptive, there is not a direct association that relates them to the privacy leakage. Within the class of metric-DP text generation mechanisms, the corresponding definition of empirical privacy-utility tradeoff is a constrained optimization to maximize the empirical privacy while keeping the utility loss under a preset budget. This constrained setup can find its precedent in the location data privacy literature (Shokri et al., 2011, 2012; Clark et al., 2019). We differ in their approach as we require the optimal mechanism to also satisfy metric-DP.

2 The Class of Vickrey Mechanisms

To motivate our construction of the Vickrey mechanisms, we begin by discussing the limitations of a general approach in the existing metric DP text generation mechanisms. We denote by $\mathcal{W} = \{w_1, \ldots, w_n\}$ the vocabulary set containing n distinct words, and by $\phi : \mathcal{W} \to \mathbb{R}^p$ a fixed embedding function that maps each word in the vocabulary set to a $p-$dimensional real vector (referred to as the embedding for the word).

A common first step is to sample an additive noise Z from a density function $p(z) \propto \exp\{-d(z, 0)\}$, where d is the distance metric used in the mechanism[2]. For example, the Laplace mechanism uses $d(x, y) = \|x - y\|_2$ (also known as Euclidean or L_2 distance), and the Mahalanobis mechanism uses $d(x, y) = \sqrt{(x - y)\Sigma^{-1}(x - y)}$ (also known as Mahalanobis distance), where Σ is the sample covariance of the word embeddings.

Once the noise is sampled, it is then added to the input word embedding and the word with an embedding that is nearest to this noised embedding is chosen as the output:

$$w_{output} = \arg\min_{w \in \mathcal{W}} d(\phi(w_{input}) + Z, w).$$

A limitation of this noisy nearest neighbor selection is that when $|Z|$ is small (in particular, smaller than half the distance from the input word to its nearest neighbor), the first nearest neighbor to the noised embedding is the same as the original input word. The problem is exaggerated for rare words, which exist in the sparse regions of the embedding space and hence, do not get perturbed even for larger noise scales. This makes it easier for an adversary to reconstruct the original word, which may contain sensitive information (*e.g.* street names).

The proposed Vickrey mechanisms generalize the noisy nearest neighbor selection step by distributing the selection probability between the first and second nearest neighbor[3] using a tuning parameter $t \in [0, 1]$ (see Algorithm 1). Intuitively, this generalization makes the reconstruction of the original input word harder (see Figures 1 and 2).

We capture our intuition for the claim above in Figure 1. For simplicity, the horizontal axis in both plots represents the one-dimensional embedding on a vocabulary containing only 5 words: (A, B, C, D, E). The vertical axis represents the output probability of each word through the mechanism. The plots represent the output probability in the mechanism for each of the 5 words, corresponding to the potential noised embedding values on the horizontal axis. The top plot represents the Laplace mechanism when only the first nearest neighbor

[2]We use the standard definition of a *metric*, which requires the distance function to satisfy (1) $d(x, x) = 0$ for all x; (2) $d(x, y) > 0$ for $y \neq x$; and, (3) the triangle inequality.

[3]See Section 5 for a general construction using k nearest neighbors and our experimental results for the same.

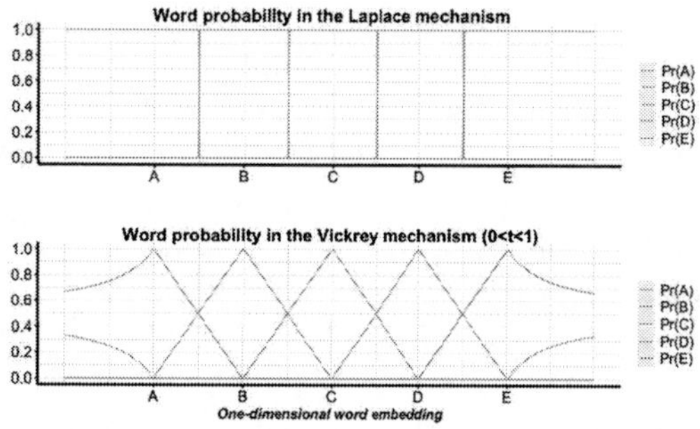

Figure 1: Word probability in the Laplace mechanism (top) and the Vickrey mechanism (bottom) at $0 < t < 1$ for each of the 5 words as a function of the noised one-dimensional embedding. The Vickrey mechanism in this example always has two candidate words as output.

Algorithm 1: The Vickrey Mechanism

Input: String $s = w_1 w_2 \dots w_n$, metric d, privacy parameter ϵ, tuning parameter $t \in [0, 1]$

for $w_i \in s$ **do**

- Sample Z with density $p(z) \propto \exp\{-\epsilon d(z, 0)\}$.
- Obtain $\hat{\phi}_i \leftarrow \phi(w_i) + Z$.
- Let $\tilde{w}_{i1} \leftarrow \underset{w \in \mathcal{W} \setminus \{w_i\}}{\arg\min} \|\hat{\phi}_i - \phi(w)\|_2$, and $\tilde{w}_{i2} \leftarrow \underset{w \in \mathcal{W} \setminus \{w_i, \tilde{w}_{i1}\}}{\arg\min} \|\hat{\phi}_i - \phi(w)\|_2$.
- Set
$$\hat{w}_i \leftarrow \begin{cases} \tilde{w}_{i1} & \text{with prob. } p(t, \hat{\phi}_i) \\ \tilde{w}_{i2} & \text{with prob. } 1 - p(t, \hat{\phi}_i) \end{cases}, \text{where}$$
$$p(t, \hat{\phi}_i) = \frac{(1-t)\|\phi(\tilde{w}_{i2}) - \hat{\phi}_i\|_2}{t\|\phi(\tilde{w}_{i1}) - \hat{\phi}_i\|_2 + (1-t)\|\phi(\tilde{w}_{i2}) - \hat{\phi}_i\|_2}.$$

return $\tilde{s} = \hat{w}_1 \hat{w}_2 \dots \hat{w}_n$.

to the noised embedding is feasible for selection ($t = 0$). In this case, all 5 curves are step functions since only the nearest neighbors are returned. The bottom plot shows the output probability for the Vickrey mechanisms, which always impart plausible deniability with another word when the noised embedding falls in any open interval.

Overview of Algorithm 1. We outline the main steps for the class of Vickrey mechanisms in Algorithm 1. For each word in the input, an additive noise Z is sampled according to the density function $p(z) \propto \exp\{-d(z, 0)\}$. Then the Vickrey mechanism will select both the first and second nearest neighbor of the noised embedding as candidates, and randomly output one of them according to probabilities calibrated by their distances to the noised embedding using a tuning parameter t. The closer t is to 1, the more the Vickrey mechanism favors the second nearest neighbor.

Privacy Analysis. We formally prove that the Vickrey mechanism M_t^ϵ at privacy parameter $\epsilon > 0$ enjoys ϵ metric-DP guarantee for any $t \in [0, 1]$.

Theorem 1. *For any $t \in [0, 1]$, $\epsilon > 0$, metric d and $w, w', \hat{w} \in \mathcal{W}$, the Vickrey mechanism M_t^ϵ from Algorithm 1 satisfies metric-DP:*

$$\frac{\Pr\{M_t^\epsilon(w) = \hat{w}\}}{\Pr\{M_t^\epsilon(w') = \hat{w}\}} \le \exp\left(\epsilon d\{\phi(w), \phi(w')\}\right).$$

Proof. Define $Q_{w_i}^{w_j} = \{v \in \mathbb{R}^p : \|v - \phi(w_i)\|_2 < \|v - \phi(w_j)\|_2 < \min_{w \in \mathcal{W} \setminus \{w_i, w_j\}} \|v - \phi(w)\|_2\}$ to be the set that has w_i and w_j as the first and second nearest neighbors. Let $p_w(z)$ be the density function for the perturbed embedding conditional on the input w:

$$p_w(z) \propto \exp\left(-\epsilon d\{z - \phi(w), 0\}\right)$$

Since metric d satisfies the triangle inequality,

$$d\{z - \phi(w'), 0\} - d\{z - \phi(w), 0\} \le d\{\phi(w), \phi(w')\},$$

we obtain:

$$e^{-\epsilon d\{z - \phi(w), 0\}} \le e^{\epsilon d\{\phi(w), \phi(w')\}} e^{-\epsilon d\{z - \phi(w'), 0\}},$$

which is equivalent to the inequality $p_w(z) \le e^{\epsilon d\{\phi(w), \phi(w')\}} p_{w'}(z)$. For brevity, let

$$\alpha_{\hat{w}}^{w_j}(t, z) = \frac{(1-t)\|z - \phi(w_j)\|_2}{t\|z - \phi(\hat{w})\|_2 + (1-t)\|z - \phi(w_j)\|_2}$$

and $\rho(w, \hat{w}) = \Pr\{M_t^\epsilon(w) = \hat{w}\}$. Since $\rho(w, \hat{w})$ is a sum of partial probabilities in the areas where $\hat{w}$ is either the first or the second nearest neighbor to the noised embedding, we have:

$$\begin{aligned} \rho(w, \hat{w}) &= \sum_{j=1} \int_{Q_{\hat{w}}^{w_j}} p_w(z) \alpha_{\hat{w}}^{w_j}(t, z) dz \\ &\quad + \sum_{i=1} \int_{Q_{w_i}^{\hat{w}}} p_w(z) \{1 - \alpha_{w_i}^{\hat{w}}(t, z)\} dz \\ &\le C(w, w') \Bigg[\sum_{j=1} \int_{Q_{\hat{w}}^{w_j}} p_{w'}(z) \alpha_{\hat{w}}^{w_j}(t, z) dz \\ &\quad + \sum_{i=1} \int_{Q_{w_i}^{\hat{w}}} p_{w'}(z) \{1 - \alpha_{w_i}^{\hat{w}}(t, z)\} dz \Bigg] \\ &= C(w, w') \Pr\{M_t^\epsilon(w') = \hat{w}\}, \end{aligned}$$

where $C(w, w') = e^{\epsilon d\{\phi(w), \phi(w')\}}$, as desired. □

For our experiments, we use the Euclidean distance for d so that the Vickrey mechanism reduces to the Laplace mechanism when $t = 0$. In general, any distance function d that satisfies the triangle inequality can be used to ensure the desired metric-DP guarantee (quantified by the parameter ϵ).

3 Tuning Parameter Selection

We now discuss how to select the tuning parameter in Algorithm 1. We do this by optimizing an empirical formulation of the privacy-utility tradeoff. We discuss the details of this formulation next.

3.1 General Framework for Empirical Privacy Utility Tradeoff

Let $M : \mathcal{W} \rightarrow \mathcal{W}$ denote some privacy-preserving text generation mechanism (that maps words to their noised versions). Define $f_M(w'|w) \triangleq \Pr\{M(w) = w'\}$ to be the probability of observing w' as the output of the mechanism M from the input word w. Note that this probability is conditioned on the knowledge of w. We assume a prior probability measure $\pi : \mathcal{W} \rightarrow [0, 1]$, which represents the adversary's domain knowledge about the NLP task and distribution of words in the dataset under consideration. Depending on the use case, the prior distribution π can be chosen as uniform, which means the user has no information on the word distribution in the context; or π can be chosen as the empirical word distribution in the corpus on which the user wishes to perform text generation.

Given this formulation, we define the expected utility loss for mechanism M as follows:

$$L_M \triangleq \sum_{w,w' \in \mathcal{W}} \pi(w) f_M(w'|w) d_L(w, w'), \quad (2)$$

where $d_L : \mathcal{W} \times \mathcal{W} \rightarrow [0, \infty)$ is a utility-specific distance metric. The utility loss can be bounded as $L_M < C$ for some bound $C > 0$, depending on the maximum tolerance for the underlying task.

To model the empirical privacy loss, we assume an informative adversary $\mathcal{A}$ that uses the prior π and has full knowledge of the text generation mechanism M and the parameter ϵ used (similar to (Shokri et al., 2011, 2012)). This adversary uses the posterior probability of each word given the observed perturbed output to make its inference:

$$g_{\mathcal{A}}(\hat{w}|w') \triangleq \frac{\pi(w') f_M(\hat{w}|w')}{\sum_{w \in \mathcal{W}} \pi(w) f_M(w'|w)}, \quad (3)$$

Thus, from $\mathcal{A}$'s perspective, the expected inference error with respect to M is given by:

$$E_M = \sum_{w,w',\hat{w}} \pi(w) f_M(w'|w) g_{\mathcal{A}}(\hat{w}|w') d_E(\hat{w}, w), \quad (4)$$

where $d_E : \mathcal{W} \times \mathcal{W} \rightarrow [0, \infty)$ is some privacy-specific distance metric. Our goal is, therefore,

Algorithm 2: Empirical Parameter Selection for the Vickrey Mechanism

Input: Vocabulary $\mathcal{W}$, maximum utility loss C, sampler for the Vickrey mechanism M_t^ϵ at any privacy parameter $\epsilon > 0$ and tuning parameter $t \in [0, 1]$
Initialize $E_{\max} \leftarrow 0, \epsilon \leftarrow \epsilon_0, t \leftarrow 0$
while $L_{M_t^\epsilon} \geq C$ **do**
  set $\epsilon = 2\epsilon$
set $E_{\max} \leftarrow E_{M_t^\epsilon}, \epsilon_{opt} \leftarrow \epsilon, t_{opt} \leftarrow 0$
for $t \in [0.05, 0.1, \ldots, 1]$ **do**
  If $L_{M_t^\epsilon} \leq C$ and $E_{M_t^\epsilon} > E_{\max}$,
    set $E_{\max} \leftarrow E_{M_t^\epsilon}, \epsilon_{opt} \leftarrow \epsilon, t_{opt} \leftarrow t$
return ϵ_{opt}, t_{opt}.

to find a mechanism within the class of metric-DP mechanisms $\mathcal{M}$ that maximizes the expected inference error E_M while keeping the utility loss L_M below C:

$$M_{\text{optimal}} = \arg\max_{M \in \mathcal{M}} E_M, \quad s.t. \ L_M < C. \quad (5)$$

To compare different mechanisms, we will compare their expected inference error E_M under different tolerance thresholds on the expected utility loss L_M. We favor mechanisms with high E_M, while maintaining $L_M < C$.

Note that d_L and d_E do not have to be the same distance metrics. For instance, d_L can depend on the downstream machine learning tasks, like the absolute difference in classification error, perplexity or even cross-entropy loss. From the privacy perspective, a natural choice is $d_E(w, \hat{w}) = \mathbb{1}(\hat{w} \neq w)$, which means the adversary attempts to retrieve the original word from the redacted output and considers the inference attack successful if the inferred word is the exactly same as the input word. Based on applications, the adversary can also choose d_E to be the Euclidean distance such that the goal of the inference attack is to have the inferred word as close to the original word as possible.

3.2 Selecting the Tuning Parameter

We outline the main steps for optimizing the privacy parameter ϵ as well as the tuning parameter t in Algorithm 2. This optimization is with respect to the empirical privacy-utility tradeoff as laid out in (5). We initialize with the privacy parameter $\epsilon = \epsilon_0$ at some small initial value ϵ_0 and tuning parameter $t = 0$, so that the initial mechanism is essentially a metric-DP mechanism that implements the noisy first nearest neighbor selection. Next, we incrementally double the value of ϵ until the expected utility loss $L_{M_t^\epsilon} < C$ (recall that a smaller ϵ typically has larger utility loss[4]). Once the maximum ϵ is obtained, we iterate over different values of t between 0 and 1 (since a monotonicity assumption cannot be made here in general for the behavior of E_M). The final parameters ϵ_{opt} and t_{opt} chosen provide the highest empirical privacy while keeping the utility loss within the specified budget. More importantly, Theorem 1 ensures that the selected mechanism enjoys at least as much metric DP as the initial mechanism, which implements only the nearest neighbor selection.

4 Experimental Results

Setup. We evaluate the performance of the proposed Vickrey mechanisms in terms of the empirical privacy-utility tradeoff on three datasets:

- The *Product Reviews dataset* consists of a list of 2,006 positive sentiment words and 4,783 negative sentiment words extracted from customer reviews (Hu and Liu, 2004). This is a word-level dataset and the metric d_L in expected utility loss is $\mathbb{1}\{\text{sentiment}(w') \neq \text{sentiment}(w)\}$, i.e., the loss is incremented when a positive sentiment word is redacted into a negative sentiment word, or vice versa.
- The *IMDb Movie Reviews dataset* (Maas et al., 2011) has a total vocabulary size of 145,901, where a pre-specified set of 26,078 words are subject to redaction in the text generation mechanism (those are the words selected for adversarial model training in (Jia et al., 2019)). The utility task is the sentence-level binary sentiment classification, where the underlying model is a bidirectional LSTM using 90% of the data for training and 10% for testing.
- The *Twitter dataset* contains 7,613 tweets, with a vocabulary of 22,013 words[5]. Each tweet is associated with a label indicating whether the tweet describes a disaster event or not. The classification model is a bidirectional LSTM using 9:1 data split for training/testing.

For all three datasets, we consider both 300-dimensional GLOVE embeddings (Pennington et al., 2014) and 300-d FASTTEXT embeddings (Bojanowski et al., 2017). The empirical privacy measurement uses the adversary's expected inference error rate, i.e. $d_E(\hat{w}, w) = \mathbb{1}(\hat{w} \neq w)$. The utility-specific metric d_L is chosen to be the misclassification error rate. The prior word distribution is chosen to be the empirical word distribution in the dataset, because we want to assume an informative adversary so as not to underestimate the privacy risk. In the Vickrey mechanism, the distance function is the Euclidean distance, so that $t = 0$ is equivalent to the Laplace mechanism (Feyisetan et al., 2020). We also compare our results with the Mahalanobis mechanism (Xu et al., 2020).

Results and Observations. In Figure 2(A) - 2(D) shows the empirical privacy-utility tradeoff on the Product Reviews between the Laplace mechanism, Mahalanobis mechanism, and the Vickrey mechanisms with tuning parameter at to 0.25, 0.5, 0.75, and 1. The vertical axis in all plots represents the adversary's inference error in the mechanism. The error bars are computed over 100 runs. In the 2(A), the horizontal axis is the privacy budget ϵ. When ϵ approaches 0, the inference error in all mechanisms approach 1, which is expected because magnitude of the additive noise is large. When ϵ increases, the inference error drops, but the drop in Laplace mechanism is much faster than the other mechanisms. It is worth noticing that the curves for Laplace mechanism and the Vickrey mechanisms are mostly parallel with each other: when t increases from 0 to 0.75, a higher value of t is better in terms of empirical privacy at the same ϵ; but when t increases to 1, the empirical privacy will not further increase since the randomness in noisy selection between the first and second nearest neighbor is replaced by the deterministic selection of the second nearest neighbor, which makes the adversary's inference attack easier by finding the second nearest neighbor. However, Vickrey mechanism at $t = 1$ still dominates Laplace mechanism which only selects the noisy first nearest neighbor for redaction. The slope for the Mahalanobis mechanism is different from the rest, where intersects with Vickrey mechanisms with different t at different ϵ. At $\epsilon = 100$, the baseline Laplace mechanism has negligible inference error, which means the adversary can almost always make correct guesses, whereas in the other mechanisms the error is still substantial.

Figure 2(B) plots inference error vs. misclassi-

[4]An implicit assumption we make in Algorithm 2 is that L_M increases monotonically with ϵ, following the intuition that a larger noise scale leads to larger utility loss. We defer the discussion around relaxing this assumption to future work.

[5]`https://www.kaggle.com/c/nlp-getting-started`

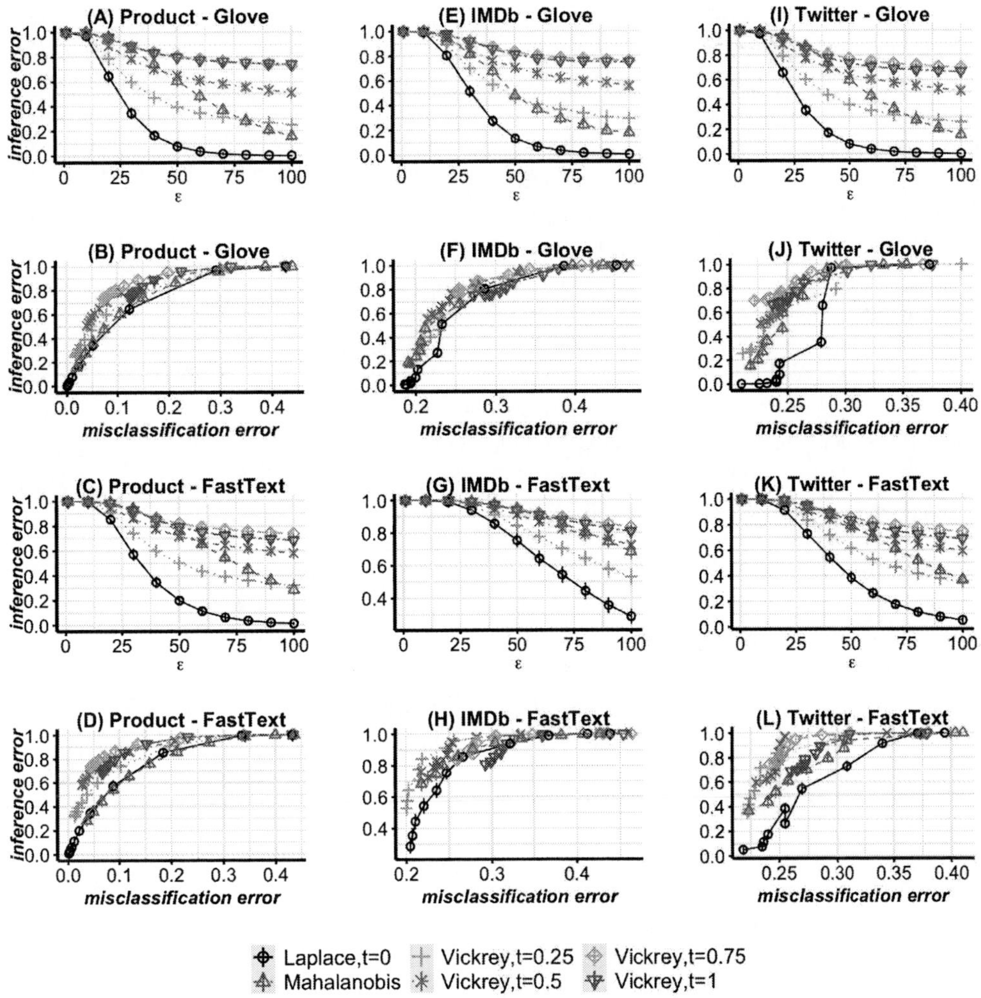

Figure 2: (A): empirical privacy vs ϵ on Product Reviews using 300-d GLOVE. (B): empirical privacy vs utility loss on Product Reviews using 300-d GLOVE. (C): empirical privacy vs ϵ on Product Reviews using 300-d FASTTEXT. (D): empirical privacy vs utility loss on Product Reviews using 300-d FASTTEXT. (E) - (H) are for IMDb reviews, and (I) - (L) are for Twitter dataset.

fication error of words (positive words to negative words, or vice versa). When vertically slicing the plot, we see that for each utility loss budget greater than 0.1, a larger value of t will result in a better privacy guarantee. When capped at a maximum $\epsilon = 100$, the curves with a higher t value will have a higher minimum feasible misclassification error, which is around around 0.02 for $t = 0.25$ and Mahalanobis, about 0.04 for $t = 0.5$, about 0.06 for $t = 0.75$, and about 0.1 for $t = 1$. This is expected because as more weight is put on the second nearest neighbor, the utility loss becomes larger at large ϵ values (small noise), because it is more likely that the original word will get changed to its neighbors. But this loss is upper bounded by the nearest neighbor replacement, which tends to be small as is shown in the experiments in the paper. The plot suggests that if the user has a maximum utility loss budget of 0.06, they should go with the Vickrey mechanism at $t = 0.75$ because when slicing vertically at misclassification error of 0.06, the green curve for $t = 0.75$ attains a higher empirical privacy than the other mechanisms. However, when the utility loss budget is 0.02, the user should choose $t = 0.25$ because the green line is on top of the other curves (red and black) that can achieve the utility loss of 0.02 (the blue, cyan, and purple curves cannot achieve utility loss within 0.02 when

ϵ is capped at 100). Figure 2(C) and 2(D) on Product Reviews using 300-d FASTTEXT embedding show similar patterns as those in 2(A) and 2(B) in terms of the privacy-utility tradeoff.

The results and interpretations are qualitative similar in Figure 2(E) - 2(H) on IMDb Movie Reviews and in Figure 2(I) - 2(L) on Twitter. In empirical privacy vs ϵ plots, the Laplace mechanism consistently has a lower value of empirical privacy measure than the Vickrey mechanism and the Mahalanobis mechanism. This gap in adversary's inference error becomes wider as ϵ increases. In the privacy vs utility loss plots, the difference between mechanisms is more significant on Twitter than on IMDb reviews. The patterns are consistent across plots, which both show that the Vickrey mechanism can improve the privacy-utility tradeoff beyond the baseline mechanism.

The difference in the result between GLOVE and FASTTEXT, particularly in 2(E) vs. 2(G) and 2(I) vs. 2(K), is due to the difference in inter-word distance distributions between the two embedding spaces (see Figure 1 in (Feyisetan et al., 2020)). In particular, the inter-word distances are generally smaller in FASTTEXT than in GLOVE, so that for a fixed noise scale ϵ, the inference error is expected to be larger in FASTTEXT than in GLOVE.

5 Generalizing Vickrey Mechanism Beyond the Second Nearest Neighbor

By a random selection of both the first and the second nearest neighbor to the noised embedding, we have shown that the Vickrey mechanism can empirically improve the privacy-utility tradeoff upon the existing Laplace and Mahalanobis mechanisms. A natural generalization is to extend the selection to $k \geq 2$ nearest neighbors (see Algorithm 3).

Algorithm 3 presents the outline of the generalized Vickrey mechanism that randomly chooses among the noisy k nearest neighbors as output, where the selection probability is inversely associated with their distance to the noised embedding. Similar to Algorithm 2, the tuning parameters are selected as to optimize for the empirical privacy-utility tradeoff, but the selection process will be more challenging because the optimization space is unbounded. We defer the details of this optimization to future work. However, we formally state in Theorem 2 the metric-DP guarantee from the generalized Vickrey mechanism in Algorithm 2. Due to space constraints, we defer the details of the proof since it is similar to that for Theorem 1.

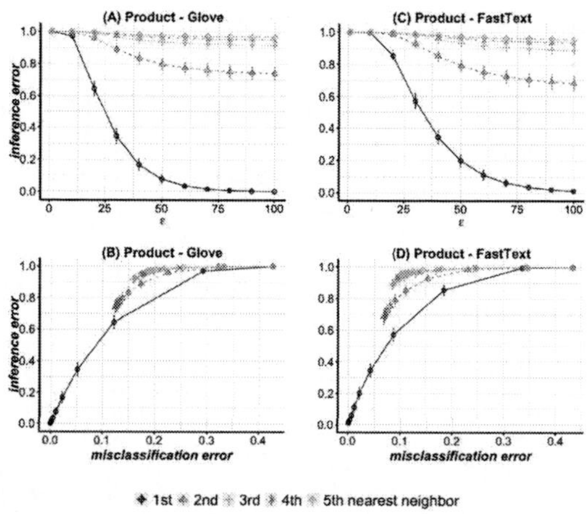

Figure 3: (A): empirical privacy vs ϵ on Product Reviews using 300-d GLOVE. (B): empirical privacy vs utility loss on Product Reviews using 300-d GLOVE. (C): empirical privacy vs ϵ on Product Reviews using 300-d FASTTEXT. (D): empirical privacy vs utility loss on Product Reviews using 300-d FASTTEXT.

Algorithm 3: Generalized Vickrey Mechanism

Input: String $s = w_1 w_2 \ldots w_n$, metric d, privacy parameter ϵ, tuning parameters $t_1, \ldots, t_k > 0$

for $w_i \in s$ **do**

  Sample Z with density $p(z) \propto \exp\{-\epsilon d(z, 0)\}$

  Obtain $\hat{\phi}_i \leftarrow \phi(w_i) + Z$

  Let $\tilde{w}_{i1} \leftarrow \underset{w \in \mathcal{W} \setminus \{w_i\}}{\arg\min} \|\hat{\phi}_i - \phi(w)\|_2$

  $\ldots$

  $\tilde{w}_{ik} \leftarrow \underset{w \in \mathcal{W} \setminus \{w_i, \tilde{w}_{i1}, \ldots, \tilde{w}_{ik}\}}{\arg\min} \|\hat{\phi}_i - \phi(w)\|_2$.

  Set $\hat{w}_i \leftarrow \tilde{w}_{ir}$ with prob. $p_r(t_{1,\ldots,k}, \hat{\phi}_i)$, where $p_r(t_{1,\ldots,k}, \hat{\phi}_i) = \frac{\exp\{-t_r \|\phi(\tilde{w}_{ir} - \hat{\phi}_i\|_2\}}{\sum_j \exp\{-t_j \|\phi(\tilde{w}_{ij} - \hat{\phi}_i\|_2\}}$ for all $r \in [k]$.

return $\tilde{s} = \hat{w}_1 \hat{w}_2 \ldots \hat{w}_n$.

Theorem 2. *For any $t = [t_1, \ldots, t_k] \in [0, \infty)^k$, $k \in \mathbb{Z}_+$, $\epsilon > 0$ and $w, w', \hat{w} \in \mathcal{W}$, the generalized Vickrey mechanism M_t^ϵ from Algorithm 3 satisfies ϵ metric-DP for any metric d.*

In Figure 3 , we compare 5 generalizations of the Vickrey mechanism that deterministically select the noisy $1^{st}, \ldots, 5^{th}$ neighbors as the output on the Product Reviews data using both 300-d GLOVE and 300-d FASTTEXT. We can see that the improvement is most significant between the 1st and 2nd nearest neighbor. It also shows that there is benefit in introducing the 3rd nearest neighbor into the selection pool, while no big difference is found beyond the 3rd neighbor.

6 Discussion and Conclusion

In this paper, we present a measurement framework to quantify the empirical privacy-utility tradeoff for metric-DP text generation mechanisms, where the empirical privacy metric is the reconstruction risk of the original text based on the redacted text. We adopt a constrained optimization setup, where within the class of metric-DP mechanisms, we maximize the empirical privacy guarantee while keeping the machine learning utility loss under a pre-specified tolerance. A novel class of Vickrey mechanism is proposed, which not only enjoys metric-DP but also optimizes the privacy-utility tradeoff within the constraint. We apply our methodology to the three text classification datasets and demonstrate how to empirically compare the privacy-utility tradeoff as well as how to choose the optimal parameter setting according to the constrained optimization. Our results show superior performance when compared to existing mechanisms.

Our analysis in this paper leaves ample room for further investigation. An ongoing work we are exploring is the inclusion of contextual information into the probability calibration between the two nearest neighbors. We leave it as an interesting open problem to explore how the choice of kth neighbor impacts the tradeoff in this scenario, since contextual signals will likely restrict the set of candidate words we can choose from.

References

Balamurugan Anandan, Chris Clifton, Wei Jiang, Mummoorthy Murugesan, Pedro Pastrana-Camacho, and Luo Si. 2012. t-plausibility: Generalizing words to desensitize text. *Trans. Data Priv.*, 5(3):505–534.

Miguel E Andrés, Nicolás E Bordenabe, Konstantinos Chatzikokolakis, and Catuscia Palamidessi. 2013. Geo-indistinguishability: Differential privacy for location-based systems. In *Proceedings of the 2013 ACM SIGSAC conference on Computer & communications security*, pages 901–914.

Piotr Bojanowski, Edouard Grave, Armand Joulin, and Tomas Mikolov. 2017. Enriching word vectors with subword information. *Transactions of the Association for Computational Linguistics*, 5:135–146.

Konstantinos Chatzikokolakis, Miguel E Andrés, Nicolás Emilio Bordenabe, and Catuscia Palamidessi. 2013. Broadening the scope of differential privacy using metrics. In *International Symposium on Privacy Enhancing Technologies Symposium*, pages 82–102. Springer.

Lillian Clark, Matthew Clark, Konstantinos Psounis, and Peter Kairouz. 2019. Privacy-utility trades in wireless data via optimization and learning.

Chad Cumby and Rayid Ghani. 2011. A machine learning based system for semi-automatically redacting documents. In *Twenty-Third IAAI Conference*.

Zeyu Ding, Yuxin Wang, Guanhong Wang, Danfeng Zhang, and Daniel Kifer. 2018. Detecting violations of differential privacy. In *Proceedings of the 2018 ACM SIGSAC Conference on Computer and Communications Security*, pages 475–489.

Josep Domingo-Ferrer, Agusti Solanas, and Jordi Castellà-Roca. 2009. h (k)-private information retrieval from privacy-uncooperative queryable databases. *Online Information Review*.

Cynthia Dwork. 2008. Differential privacy: A survey of results. In *International conference on theory and applications of models of computation*, pages 1–19. Springer.

Cynthia Dwork, Frank McSherry, Kobbi Nissim, and Adam Smith. 2006. Calibrating noise to sensitivity in private data analysis. In *Theory of cryptography conference*, pages 265–284. Springer.

Cynthia Dwork, Aaron Roth, et al. 2014. The algorithmic foundations of differential privacy. *Foundations and Trends in Theoretical Computer Science*, 9(3-4):211–407.

Natasha Fernandes, Mark Dras, and Annabelle McIver. 2019. Generalised differential privacy for text document processing. In *International Conference on Principles of Security and Trust*, pages 123–148. Springer, Cham.

Oluwaseyi Feyisetan, Borja Balle, Thomas Drake, and Tom Diethe. 2020. Privacy-and utility-preserving textual analysis via calibrated multivariate perturbations. In *Proceedings of the 13th International Conference on Web Search and Data Mining*, pages 178–186.

Oluwaseyi Feyisetan, Tom Diethe, and Thomas Drake. 2019. Leveraging hierarchical representations for preserving privacy and utility in text. In *2019 IEEE International Conference on Data Mining (ICDM)*, pages 210–219. IEEE.

Anna C Gilbert and Audra McMillan. 2018. Property testing for differential privacy. In *2018 56th Annual Allerton Conference on Communication, Control, and Computing (Allerton)*, pages 249–258. IEEE.

Minqing Hu and Bing Liu. 2004. Mining and summarizing customer reviews. In *Proceedings of the tenth ACM SIGKDD international conference on Knowledge discovery and data mining*, pages 168–177.

Robin Jia, Aditi Raghunathan, Kerem Göksel, and Percy Liang. 2019. Certified robustness to adversarial word substitutions. *arXiv preprint arXiv:1909.00986*.

Shiva Prasad Kasiviswanathan, Homin K Lee, Kobbi Nissim, Sofya Raskhodnikova, and Adam Smith. 2011. What can we learn privately? *SIAM Journal on Computing*, 40(3):793–826.

Aleksandra Korolova, Krishnaram Kenthapadi, Nina Mishra, and Alexandros Ntoulas. 2009. Releasing search queries and clicks privately. In *Proceedings of the 18th international conference on World wide web*, pages 171–180.

Peeter Laud, Alisa Pankova, and Martin Pettai. 2020. A framework of metrics for differential privacy from local sensitivity. *Proceedings on Privacy Enhancing Technologies*, 2020(2):175–208.

Ninghui Li, Tiancheng Li, and Suresh Venkatasubramanian. 2007. t-closeness: Privacy beyond k-anonymity and l-diversity. In *2007 IEEE 23rd International Conference on Data Engineering*, pages 106–115. IEEE.

Xiyang Liu and Sewoong Oh. 2019. Minimax rates of estimating approximate differential privacy. *arXiv preprint arXiv:1905.10335*.

Andrew Maas, Raymond E Daly, Peter T Pham, Dan Huang, Andrew Y Ng, and Christopher Potts. 2011. Learning word vectors for sentiment analysis. In *Proceedings of the 49th annual meeting of the association for computational linguistics: Human language technologies*, pages 142–150.

Ashwin Machanavajjhala, Daniel Kifer, Johannes Gehrke, and Muthuramakrishnan Venkitasubramaniam. 2007. l-diversity: Privacy beyond k-anonymity. *ACM Transactions on Knowledge Discovery from Data (TKDD)*, 1(1):3–es.

Hwee Hwa Pang, Xuhua Ding, and Xiaokui Xiao. 2010. Embellishing text search queries to protect user privacy.

Jeffrey Pennington, Richard Socher, and Christopher D Manning. 2014. Glove: Global vectors for word representation. In *Proceedings of the 2014 conference on empirical methods in natural language processing (EMNLP)*, pages 1532–1543.

Albin Petit, Thomas Cerqueus, Sonia Ben Mokhtar, Lionel Brunie, and Harald Kosch. 2015. Peas: Private, efficient and accurate web search. In *2015 IEEE Trustcom/BigDataSE/ISPA*, volume 1, pages 571–580. IEEE.

Ahmed Salem, Yang Zhang, Mathias Humbert, Pascal Berrang, Mario Fritz, and Michael Backes. 2018. Ml-leaks: Model and data independent membership inference attacks and defenses on machine learning models. *arXiv preprint arXiv:1806.01246*.

David Sánchez and Montserrat Batet. 2016. C-sanitized: A privacy model for document redaction and sanitization. *Journal of the Association for Information Science and Technology*, 67(1):148–163.

David Sánchez, Jordi Castellà-Roca, and Alexandre Viejo. 2013. Knowledge-based scheme to create privacy-preserving but semantically-related queries for web search engines. *Information Sciences*, 218:17–30.

Reza Shokri, Marco Stronati, Congzheng Song, and Vitaly Shmatikov. 2017. Membership inference attacks against machine learning models. In *2017 IEEE Symposium on Security and Privacy (SP)*, pages 3–18. IEEE.

Reza Shokri, George Theodorakopoulos, Jean-Yves Le Boudec, and Jean-Pierre Hubaux. 2011. Quantifying location privacy. In *2011 IEEE symposium on security and privacy*, pages 247–262. IEEE.

Reza Shokri, George Theodorakopoulos, Carmela Troncoso, Jean-Pierre Hubaux, and Jean-Yves Le Boudec. 2012. Protecting location privacy: optimal strategy against localization attacks. In *Proceedings of the 2012 ACM conference on Computer and communications security*, pages 617–627.

Congzheng Song and Vitaly Shmatikov. 2019. Auditing data provenance in text-generation models. In *Proceedings of the 25th ACM SIGKDD International Conference on Knowledge Discovery & Data Mining*, pages 196–206.

Latanya Sweeney. 2002. k-anonymity: A model for protecting privacy. *International Journal of Uncertainty, Fuzziness and Knowledge-Based Systems*, 10(05):557–570.

William Vickrey. 1961. Counterspeculation, auctions, and competitive sealed tenders. *The Journal of finance*, 16(1):8–37.

Zekun Xu, Abhinav Aggarwal, Oluwaseyi Feyisetan, and Nathanael Teissier. 2020. A differentially private text perturbation method using a regularized mahalanobis metric. In *Proceedings of the Workshop on PrivateNLP at the 2020 conference on empirical methods in natural language processing (EMNLP)*.

Samuel Yeom, Irene Giacomelli, Matt Fredrikson, and Somesh Jha. 2018. Privacy risk in machine learning: Analyzing the connection to overfitting. In *2018 IEEE 31st Computer Security Foundations Symposium (CSF)*, pages 268–282. IEEE.

Learning and Evaluating a Differentially Private Pre-trained Language Model

Shlomo Hoory,* Amir Feder, Avichai Tendler, Alon Cohen, Sofia Erell, Itay Laish, Hootan Nakhost, Uri Stemmer, Ayelet Benjamini, Avinatan Hassidim and Yossi Matias
Google
Tel Aviv, Israel
{afeder,tendler,aloncohen,rovinsky}@google.com

Abstract

Contextual language models have led to significantly better results on a plethora of language understanding tasks, especially when pre-trained on the same data as the downstream task. While this additional pre-training usually improves performance, it can lead to information leakage and therefore risks the privacy of individuals mentioned in the training data. One method to guarantee the privacy of such individuals is to train a differentially-private model, but this usually comes at the expense of model performance. Moreover, it is hard to tell given a privacy parameter ϵ what was the effect on the trained representation. In this work we aim to guide future practitioners and researchers on how to improve privacy while maintaining good model performance. We demonstrate how to train a differentially-private pre-trained language model (i.e., BERT) with a privacy guarantee of $\epsilon = 1$ and with only a small degradation in performance. We experiment on a dataset of clinical notes with a model trained on a target entity extraction task, and compare it to a similar model trained without differential privacy. Finally, we present experiments showing how to interpret the differentially-private representation and understand the information lost and maintained in this process.

1 Introduction

Recent advancements in natural language processing (NLP), mainly the introduction of the transformer architecture and contextual language representations, have led to a surge in the performance and applicability language models. Such models rely on pre-training on massive self-labeled corpora to incorporate knowledge within the language representation. Additionally, when presented with a new dataset and task, such models often gain from an additional pre-training stage, where they are trained to solve a language modeling task on the new training data.

While the pre-training steps are crucial for good model performance on downstream tasks, it can come at the expense of the privacy of the persons mentioned in the data. As these models learn to predict words using their context, they often memorize individual words and phrases. Such memorization can lead to information leakage when using the trained models or the language representation. This problem is amplified in medical domains, where patients data might leak and expose Protected Health Information (PHI).

One solution for pre-training the model while preserving patients' privacy is to train the model with a differential privacy guarantee. However, for a sufficiently small privacy parameter ϵ, this usually comes at the expense of model performance. Also, it was only shown to work for recurrent language models, and not for more recent systems that are based on the transformer architecture (McMahan et al., 2018; Kerrigan et al., 2020). Apart from their size (our model has 109M trainable parameters), transformer-based language models introduce an additional privacy concern, as their reliance on WordPiece based tokenization algorithm can also potentially leak private information.

Moreover, even with a sufficiently small ϵ guarantee, it is hard to test and evaluate the resulting privacy-preserving properties of the model. One also has difficulty understanding whether the differentially-private training procedure affected the language representation other than by measuring performance on a downstream task. For example, it could be that other valuable information was also lost during training.

In this work we provide here a detailed solution to training a differentially-private contextual embedding model, and to better understand the resulting representation. We start by presenting a method for training BERT, a contextual embedding

*Work was done while at Google.

Proceedings of the 58th Annual Meeting of the Association for Computational Linguistics, pages 21–29
July 5–10, 2020. ©2020 Association for Computational Linguistics
https://doi.org/10.26615/978-954-452-056-4_003

model, on medical data with a strong privacy guarantee of $\epsilon = 1$ and with only a small degradation in performance (Section 3). Possibly the most major technical challenge in doing so is the fact that the training batch size has to be fairly large, all the while training on specific hardware (TPUs) in which the batch size is limited. We overcome this obstacle by distributing each training batch over time during the training process, along with other useful manipulations (Section 2.1). As these models gain from retraining the WordPiece algorithm on the target dataset, we propose a differentially-private WordPiece algorithm, preventing additional information leakage through the model's vocabulary (Section 3.2).

After training the differentially-private BERT on clinical notes, we follow common wisdom and provide privacy tests to show that information leakage has been prevented in this process (Section 5). We further provide adversarial attacks that can help understand the privacy guarantees in terms of memorized words and phrases. These tests, when combined, provide a useful toolbox for understanding how "private" is the differentially-private model.

2 Previous Work

Since the introduction of the differentially-private Stochastic Gradient Descent (SGD) algorithm (Song et al., 2013; Abadi et al., 2016b), it is possible to train deep neural networks (DNN) with privacy guarantees. Specifically, there have been several attempts to train DNN-based language models with such guarantees, though with mixed results in terms of performance on downstream tasks (McMahan et al., 2018; Kerrigan et al., 2020). To better understand the trade-offs between the performance and privacy of deep language models, we survey here the literature on differentially-private training and on methods for measuring privacy in language models.

2.1 Training Differentially-Private Models

Differential Privacy (DP; Dwork et al., 2006b; Dwork, 2011; Dwork et al., 2014) is a framework that quantifies the privacy leaked by some randomized algorithm accessing a private dataset. In the context of training a machine learning model on private data, it enables one to bound the potential privacy leakage by releasing the model to the world.

Definition 1 (**(ϵ, δ)-DP**) *Given some $\epsilon, \delta > 0$, we say that algorithm $\mathcal{A}$ has (ϵ, δ)-differential privacy, if for any two datasets D, D' differing in a single element and for all $S \subseteq Range(\mathcal{A})$, we have:*

$$\Pr[\mathcal{A}(D) \in S] \leq e^{\epsilon} \Pr[\mathcal{A}(D') \in S] + \delta.$$

The leading method for training models with small differential privacy parameters ϵ, δ is the DP-SGD method by Abadi et al. (2016b). The method was subsequently incorporated into Tensorflow's privacy toolbox with improved privacy analysis (Mironov, 2017; Mironov et al., 2019). The basic idea behind DP-SGD is to clip and add noise to the per example gradients of the loss function during model training. The intuition is that such a mechanism guarantees that, for each step, the influence of each example on the outcome is bounded.

In the context of NLP, there have been several attempts to train language models using the DP-SGD algorithm. Specifically, McMahan et al. (2018) presented a pipeline for training differentially-private language models based on the recurrent neural network (RNN) architecture. While successful on the RNN architecture, results on a fine-tuned transformer, specifically GPT-2, were shown to be less successful in preserving privacy without hurting task performance (Kerrigan et al., 2020). In this paper, we present the first, as far as we know, successfully trained differentially private BERT model, with a strong privacy guarantee and with only a small decrease in downstream performance.

2.2 Evaluating the Privacy of Language Models

While differential privacy training provides privacy guarantees (in terms of the privacy parameters ϵ, δ), it is often hard to evaluate the practical implication of such a guarantee. In the context of language models, evaluation becomes even trickier. Private information might be encoded in specific phrases contained in the text, but it can also be implicitly contained in the language model. In the context of clinical notes, for example, information regarding the linguistic style of the doctor can be captured and predicted from linguistic cues in the text itself (Rosenthal and McKeown, 2011; Preoţiuc-Pietro et al., 2015; Coavoux et al., 2018).

Song and Raghunathan (2020) studied information leakage from language representations, and presented several methods for evaluating the privacy preserving qualities of trained language models. They provided a taxonomy of adversarial attacks, differing by the adversary's access to model's internal state. Specifically, they defined membership attacks on language representation, which are designed to detect memorized information. In this paper, we build on the secret sharer membership test, a method for quantitatively assessing the risk that rare or unique training-data sequences are unintentionally memorized by generative sequence models (Carlini et al., 2019). While not specifically designed for language models such as BERT, it fits the DP evaluation setup perfectly. Concretely, in this test a secret sharer plants n identical occurrences of a k WordPiece sequence into the train corpus. The sequence itself consists of i.i.d. random WordPieces where the middle is the secret. The model is then trained on the modified corpus and evaluated for each planted sequence by trying to predict the secret WordPiece.

In Section 5, we show that unlike the original BERT model, our trained DP-BERT model does not memorize sequences of words introduced via the secret sharer.

3 Training Differentially Private Contextual Language Models

Training differentially private language models becomes exceedingly difficult with model size. As such, attempting to train a transformer model such as BERT using the DP-SGD algorithm and without any modifications will usually lead to a significant performance degradation (Kerrigan et al., 2020). Moreover, as the WordPiece algorithm, the process that tokenizes the textual input of BERT, is not differentially private, training will not guarantee that there is no information leakage. In this section, we formulate the problem of training a DP BERT model on medical text, and explain the process of constructing a differentially private vocabulary. We then discuss the importance of parallel training and very large batch sizes in training such large language models, and provide a method for sufficiently increasing such crucial parameters.

3.1 Problem Formulation

We choose to focus our DP training on the task of entity extraction (EE) from medical text, specifically clinical notes. Clinical notes include medically relevant information regarding patients' conditions, and are often used as training data for downstream machine learning tasks (Esteva et al., 2019). However, they can contain Protected Health Information (PHI) as well as additional information that might put patients at risk (Feder et al., 2020; Hartman et al., 2020). For this reason, language models trained on such datasets must be able to learn domain-relevant information (such as medical jargon and doctors' writing style) without memorizing private information (Lee et al., 2020).

To test our ability to train a DP language model on clinical notes, we use a BERT model (Devlin et al., 2019) with specialization to the medical domain. To this end, the public Wikipedia and BookCorpus datasets (Zhu et al., 2015) used to train BERT were amended with the Medical Information Mart for Intensive Care III corpus (Johnson et al., 2016, MIMIC-III) in order to improve performance on medical tasks. Although MIMIC-III has undergone a de-identification process aimed to remove revealing information such as names and dates, the corpus and its derivative models are not considered public, and their use must adhere to certain restrictions. As a consequence, a need arises to build a medical BERT model with substantial differential privacy guarantees on its use of MIMIC-III, and this work aims to do exactly that.

Before introducing changes designed to guarantee privacy, let us review the procedure used to obtain the Medical BERT model. The available resources are the 3 billion word Wikipedia + BookCorpus, and the 712M word MIMIC-III corpus. The training process consists of the following three steps:

(i) Build the vocab from the MIMIC-III corpus.

(ii) Train BERT from scratch on the Wikipedia + BookCorpus using the new vocab.

(iii) Continue BERT's training on the MIMIC-III corpus.

The steps that are susceptible to leaking MIMIC-III data are the first, and the third. Therefore, by the composability property of differential privacy (Dwork et al., 2014, Theorem 3.16), our problem reduces to providing algorithms with satisfactory DP guarantees for steps 1 and 3 without causing a significant performance loss. We discuss these problems in the following two subsections.

3.2 Constructing a differentially private vocabulary

Transformer-based models commonly tokenize inputs into WordPieces using the WordPiece algorithm. The WordPiece algorithm (Wu et al., 2016) is a general method for improving the generalization properties of a language model by tokenizing based on the most frequent combination of symbols rather than words. While its efficacy is undisputed, it can leak private information by memorizing certain WordPieces in the training data. To prevent such leakage, we modify this algorithm to be differentially private. We do so as follows.

The WordPiece algorithm starts with constructing the word histogram of the corpus. This histogram is then manipulated to obtain the WordPiece output vocabulary. Since differential privacy is robust to post-processing, it is enough to make the input histogram differentially private in order to guarantee a differentially-private end-result vocabulary. Our differentially-private WordPiece algorithm is therefore to add noise to the histogram with given privacy parameters and apply the standard WordPiece algorithm.

Histogram noising is done following (Korolova et al., 2009; Bun et al., 2019), let X be the set of all possible n distinct words. For the input histogram $h : X \rightarrow \mathbb{R}$, we do:

(i) For all $x \in X$, if $h(x) > 0$, add Laplace noise: $h(x) \leftarrow h(x) + \text{Lap}(2/\epsilon)$.

(ii) For all $x \in X$, if $h(x) < 1 + 2\ln(2/\delta)/\epsilon$, set $h(x) \leftarrow 0$.

The output h of this process satisfies (ϵ, δ)-differential privacy with respect to replacing one of the words in the histogram counts. Assuming $0 < \epsilon < ln(n)$, $0 < \delta < 1/n$ (Bun et al., 2019; Korolova et al., 2009).

In order to obtain differential privacy at the level of BERT example (256???? WordPiece) we use the basic composition theorem for non-adaptive queries (Dwork et al., 2006a; Dwork and Lei, 2009):

Theorem 1 *Let $M_1, \ldots M_k$ be (ϵ, δ)-differentially private, then $(M_1, \ldots, M_k)$ is $(k\epsilon, k\delta)$-differentially private.*

We used parameters $\epsilon' =?, \delta' =??$ in the noisy histogram algorithm above to achieve an example level $(\epsilon = 256*?, \delta = 256*?)$ differential privacy.

3.3 Training a differentially private BERT

We use the DP-SGD method supplied the TF privacy toolbox (see Section 2.1). The parameters of the algorithm are the number of steps, batch-size B, ℓ_2-norm-clip C, and the noise multiplier σ. To fix notation, we formally define the DP-SGD step, as defined in Abadi et al. (2016b, Algorithm 1). Given the per-example gradients of the loss function $g_1, \ldots, g_B$, the gradient $\tilde{g}$ for passing to `apply_gradients` is defined by:

$$\overline{g_i} = g_i / \max(1, \|g_i\|_2 / C), \quad \text{for all } i; \tag{1}$$

$$\tilde{g} = \frac{1}{B}\left(\sum_i \overline{g_i} + \mathcal{N}(0, \sigma^2 C^2 \mathbb{I})\right). \tag{2}$$

The most important parameter of the algorithm is the noise multiplier σ—increasing σ directly decreases ϵ; i.e., increases the differential-privacy guarantee of the algorithm. On the other hand it harms performance on the target data-set, and thus a careful choice of σ is necessary to trade-off privacy against performance. Moreover, we choose the noise σ to be proportional to the square root of the batch size B. This is done in order to make the privacy guarantee oblivious to changes in the batch size B (as one can observe from Eq. (2)). The privacy guarantee is also affected by the number of training steps (or epochs), but this behavior is more gradual since ϵ increases near-linearly in the range of interest. In our experience, the clip level C is of lesser importance and we fix it to be 0.01.

For any choice of parameters, we upper bound the privacy parameter ϵ using the TF privacy toolbox `compute_dp_sgd_privacy` function, where we also use the number of MIMIC examples $N = 83M$. We fix privacy δ to be 10^{-8}, which is smaller than $1/N$.

The effect of parallelism. In order to make the training run faster, we use TPUs[1] to parallelize training by splitting example batches to shards. This mechanism is readily available through Tensorflow (TF; Abadi et al., 2016a), but its effect has to be taken into account when computing the bounds on ϵ.

In order to understand this effect, let us first review the way we incorporate TF privacy into the BERT training code. The change consists of changing the loss computation code to compute the vector loss (per-example loss), and of wrapping the existing Adam weight decay optimizer (Kingma and Ba, 2015), our optimizer of choice, by the DP optimizer using the `make_gaussian_optimizer_class` method.

The subtle point lies in the second change, as the optimization is also wrapped by `CrossShardOptimizer` which handles the sharded batching. Let B denote the unsharded

[1] `https://cloud.google.com/tpu/docs/tpus.`

batch size, and P denote the number of parallel shards. For each batch, the examples are split between P independent instances of the TF privacy optimizer, each handling B/P examples. For each shard, the gradients are clipped, averaged and noise is added by equations Eqs. (1) and (2). Subsequently, the `CrossShardOptimizer` averages the P shard gradients to obtain the single gradient to be passed to `apply_gradients`.

Therefore, denoting the i-th gradient of shard j by $g_{i,j}$, the gradient passed to `apply_gradients` can be written as follows:

$$\tilde{g} = \frac{1}{P}\sum_j \left[\frac{1}{B/P}\left(\sum_i \overline{g_{i,j}} + \mathcal{N}(0, \sigma^2 C^2 \mathbb{I})\right)\right]$$
$$= \frac{1}{B}\left(\sum_{i,j} \overline{g_{i,j}} + \mathcal{N}(0, P\sigma^2 C^2 \mathbb{I})\right). \quad (3)$$

This implies that using noise multiplier σ with P shards is equivalent to an unsharded training with noise multiplier $\sigma\sqrt{P}$. As computing an upper bound on ϵ through TF privacy does not take parallelism into account, one must use $\sigma\sqrt{P}$ as the noise multiplier in order to get the correct result.

Achieving larger batch sizes. As it quickly became apparent throughout this project, we needed larger batch sizes. However, usually batch size cannot increase beyond a certain point because of memory considerations, and limitation on the number of available TPUs. With the resources available to us, we couldn't get beyond parallelism of $P = 256$ with sharded batch size of 32, achieving total batch size $B = 8192$.

The way we chose to solve this problem is to spread the batch in time, so `apply_gradients` is called only after T batches are processed with the average total gradient. This is equivalent to increasing both P and B by a factor of T. With this method, the only limit on T is processing time. From our experience, the value of $T = 32$ is a reasonable choice, achieving parallelism of $P = 256 \cdot 32$ and total batch size B of 128k with the above parameters.

We briefly remark upon the implementation of this mechanism. For every trainable variable, we created a variable with `/grad_acc` suffix added to the original name. For each step, the `train_op` either accumulates the current gradients in the new variables, or zeros the accumulator and calls `apply_gradients`, depending on the current step modulo T.

4 Experimental Setup

We design our experiments to demonstrate the ability of the DP training scheme to improve performance while preserving privacy. We focus on the medical domain as it has strict privacy requirements and its language is distinct enough such that additional pre-training should be useful. We start by describing the data used for the DP training and relevant implementation details. We then present the entity extraction task used for the supervised task training and evaluation. Finally, we discuss the relevant baselines, chosen to demonstrate the efficacy of the DP training scheme.

Pre-training data. For the DP pre-training, we supplement the original training data used in Devlin et al. (2019) with the MIMIC-III dataset, a commonly used collection of medical information that contains more than 2 million distinct notes (Johnson et al., 2016; Alsentzer et al., 2019). MIMIC-III covers 38,597 distinct adult patients and 49,785 hospital admissions between 2001 and 2012. The clinical notes in this dataset are widely used by NLP researchers for a variety of clinically-related tasks (Feder et al., 2020; Hartman et al., 2020), and were previously used for pre-training BERT models specifically for the medical domain (Alsentzer et al., 2019).

Using the combined dataset, we train our DP-BERT model using the the training scheme described in Section 3. At this point, we use a WordPiece vocabulary generated from MIMIC-III without privacy guarantees.

Entity-extraction task. For the supervised task training, we use i2b2-2010, a dataset from the i2b2 National Center for Biomedical Computing for the NLP Shared Tasks Challenges (Uzuner et al., 2011). This dataset contains clinical notes tagged for concepts, assertions, and relations. In this task, 170 patient reports are labeled with three concepts: test, treatment, and problem. The total number of entities in each category are as follows:

- Problem: 7,073
- Test: 4,608
- Treatment: 4,844

We perform 5-fold cross validation where each fold has random training (136 notes) and test (34 notes) sets.

Baselines. We compare our differentially private BERT model, denoted as DP BERT, to several non private baselines:

BERT (Wikipedia + Books) We train a BERT-large model, as in Devlin et al. (2019), using the default hyperparameters.

BERT-M (Wikipedia + Books + MIMIC-III) We supplement the original training from Devlin et al. (2019) with the MIMIC-III clinical notes corpus. In addition, we also use a (non-differentially private) WordPiece vocabulary generated from MIMIC-III.

BioBERT We use the training data presented in Lee et al. (2020), and use it to train BERT. We tested version v1.1 which it trained using the original dataset + 1M PubMed abstracts.

In Section 5 we compare several differentially private models, discuss their differences and highlight the effect of certain parameters (as discussed in Section 3) on the EE task performance.

5 Results

In this section we empirically evaluate the trade-offs between a model's privacy and its usefulness. Previously, in Section 3, we have shown how to pre-train a contextual embedding model such as BERT with any, possibly substantial, privacy guarantee. We naturally expect that a stronger privacy guarantee would entail that less information is preserved during pre-training, which in turn would degrade performance on downstream tasks. Thus, we aim to ascertain the exact trade-off between these two goals in order to be able to choose a model that has both good performance and a satisfactory privacy guarantee.

We provide two sets of experiments to help better understand this trade-off as well as to provide practitioners with tools to understand the effects of DP pre-training. First, we use the pre-trained DP model and fine-tune it on the aforementioned EE task. Then, we test the ability of the model to memorize private information and show that it is protected against commonly used privacy attacks. Aggregating both results, we argue that medically-relevant information is preserved in the DP model all the while private information is not revealed.

5.1 Preserving Useful Information

For our first experiment, we pre-trained a DP BERT model, then evaluated on an EE task over the i2b2-2010 dataset. We summarize our results in the following table.

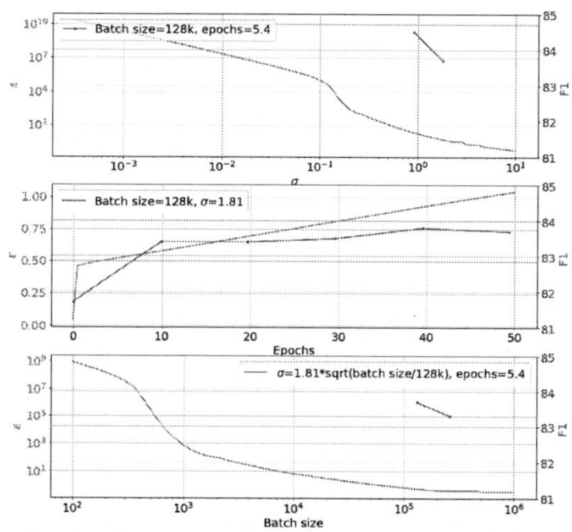

Figure 1: Top to bottom - privacy parameter ϵ (red) and test F1 score on the EE task (blue), as a function of: noise multiplier σ; number of pre-training epochs; pre-training batch size.

Model	ϵ	F1 Score
BERT	∞	76.3%
BERT-M	∞	86.8%
BioBERT	∞	86.5%
BERT-M	3.2	84.5%
BERT-M	1	83.7%

Table 1: Results on the Medical Entity Extraction task. $\epsilon = \infty$ means no differential privacy.

These were all evaluated after 1M training steps with batch size 128K. As one can observe, the additional pre-training either on MIMIC-III or on PubMed gives a significant boost in performance over the off-the-shelf BERT. The addition of differential privacy then deteriorates performance only slightly, and, as expected, performance is inversely proportional to ϵ (recall that smaller ϵ implies better privacy).

In addition, in Fig. 1 we evaluate the change in ϵ and of the F1 score of the downstream task as a function of batch size, noise multiplier σ, and the number of pre-training epochs. The behavior in all three parameters is as expected. Increasing σ enables more privacy (lower ϵ), but worsens performance. Similarly, with more pre-training epochs the model gathers more information about the training data, so we obtain better F1 score but worse privacy preservation (higher ϵ). When increasing the batch size, we also increase the noise multiplier

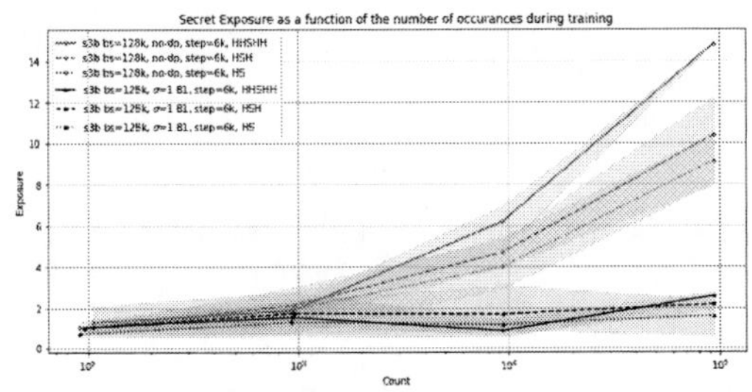

Figure 2: Secret exposure as a function of the number of secret occurrences. Black lines for models with differential privacy $\epsilon = 0.58$, red lines for models without DP $\epsilon = \infty$.

σ proportionally, thus both ϵ and the F1 decrease.

5.2 Forgetting Private Information

For our second experiment, we followed Carlini et al. (2019) to test the model's ability to memorize private information. We injected the MIMIC-III dataset with "secrets", of the form HS, HSH, and HHSHH, where H is a generic word and S is a secret word. The injection was done by sampling locations to plant each secret uniformly at random from the dataset. We tested all three forms of secrets on a DP model and a non-DP model, with different numbers of appearances of the secret in the dataset. For each such evaluation, we measured the exposure of the secret which essentially measures how well the model memorized the secret (see Carlini et al., 2019 for exact definition of "exposure"). As one can see from Fig. 2, even when the secret appears as much as 100K times in the data, the DP model performs significantly better than without differential privacy. This seems to suggest that the model learns through information that helps it generalize rather than memorizing the dataset in its entirety, which includes private and personal information as well.

6 Discussion and Future Work

In this paper, we have shown a pipeline for learning and evaluating a differentially-private contextual language model. We have defined the problem of learning such a model with end-to-end privacy guarantees and have discussed the pitfalls that might lead to poor downstream performance. To overcome the difficulties associated with learning such models, we have offered practical measures for circumventing them, most notably through vastly increasing batch sizes. Then, to increase the trust of the DP trained contextual language model, we have utilized a secret sharer evaluation test and showed that our trained language model does not memorize private information.

While these results are definitely encouraging, more research is needed. Our results are confined to the medical domain, where privacy needs are perhaps most stringent. Showing the efficacy of this training and evaluation pipeline on other domains would certainly increase the trust in it. Additionally, we have not yet measured the model's performance with the DP WordPiece algorithm. In future work, we plan to provide more theoretical and empirical support for end-to-end privacy guarantees.

Finally, the observed performance gain due to the vocabulary training presents an interesting question for the larger NLP community. Understanding the importance of vocabulary vs. linguistic style when performing additional pre-training could improve the domain adaptation capabilities of existing NLP systems. In future work, we plan to expand our DP training to additional domains, allowing us to test the power of vocabulary modifications via the DP WordPiece training in increasing across domain performance.

References

Martín Abadi, Ashish Agarwal, Paul Barham, Eugene Brevdo, Zhifeng Chen, Craig Citro, Greg S Corrado, Andy Davis, Jeffrey Dean, Matthieu Devin, et al. 2016a. Tensorflow: Large-scale machine learning on heterogeneous distributed systems. *arXiv preprint arXiv:1603.04467*.

Martin Abadi, Andy Chu, Ian Goodfellow, H Brendan McMahan, Ilya Mironov, Kunal Talwar, and Li Zhang. 2016b. Deep learning with differential privacy. In *Proceedings of the 2016 ACM SIGSAC Conference on Computer and Communications Security*, pages 308–318.

Emily Alsentzer, John R Murphy, Willie Boag, Wei-Hung Weng, Di Jin, Tristan Naumann, WA Redmond, and Matthew BA McDermott. 2019. Publicly available clinical bert embeddings. *NAACL HLT 2019*, page 72.

Mark Bun, Kobbi Nissim, and Uri Stemmer. 2019. Simultaneous private learning of multiple concepts. *J. Mach. Learn. Res.*, 20:94–1.

Nicholas Carlini, Chang Liu, Úlfar Erlingsson, Jernej Kos, and Dawn Song. 2019. The secret sharer: Evaluating and testing unintended memorization in neural networks. In *28th {USENIX} Security Symposium ({USENIX} Security 19)*, pages 267–284.

Maximin Coavoux, Shashi Narayan, and Shay B Cohen. 2018. Privacy-preserving neural representations of text. In *Proceedings of the 2018 Conference on Empirical Methods in Natural Language Processing*, pages 1–10.

Jacob Devlin, Ming-Wei Chang, Kenton Lee, and Kristina Toutanova. 2019. BERT: Pre-training of deep bidirectional transformers for language understanding. In *Proceedings of the 2019 Conference of the North American Chapter of the Association for Computational Linguistics: Human Language Technologies, Volume 1 (Long and Short Papers)*, pages 4171–4186, Minneapolis, Minnesota. Association for Computational Linguistics.

Cynthia Dwork. 2011. A firm foundation for private data analysis. *Communications of the ACM*, 54(1):86–95.

Cynthia Dwork, Krishnaram Kenthapadi, Frank McSherry, Ilya Mironov, and Moni Naor. 2006a. Our data, ourselves: privacy via distributed noise generation. In *Advances in Cryptology - EUROCRYPT 2006*, pages 486–503. Springer.

Cynthia Dwork and Jing Lei. 2009. Differential privacy and robust statistics. In *Proceedings of the Forty-First Annual ACM Symposium on Theory of Computing*, pages 371–380. Association for Computing Machinery.

Cynthia Dwork, Frank McSherry, Kobbi Nissim, and Adam Smith. 2006b. Calibrating noise to sensitivity in private data analysis. In *Theory of cryptography conference*, pages 265–284. Springer.

Cynthia Dwork, Aaron Roth, et al. 2014. The algorithmic foundations of differential privacy. *Foundations and Trends in Theoretical Computer Science*, 9(3-4):211–407.

Andre Esteva, Alexandre Robicquet, Bharath Ramsundar, Volodymyr Kuleshov, Mark DePristo, Katherine Chou, Claire Cui, Greg Corrado, Sebastian Thrun, and Jeff Dean. 2019. A guide to deep learning in healthcare. *Nature medicine*, 25(1):24–29.

Amir Feder, Danny Vainstein, Roni Rosenfeld, Tzvika Hartman, Avinatan Hassidim, and Yossi Matias. 2020. Active deep learning to detect demographic traits in free-form clinical notes. *Journal of Biomedical Informatics*, 107:103436.

Tzvika Hartman, Michael D Howell, Jeff Dean, Shlomo Hoory, Ronit Slyper, Itay Laish, Oren Gilon, Danny Vainstein, Greg Corrado, Katherine Chou, et al. 2020. Customization scenarios for de-identification of clinical notes. *BMC medical informatics and decision making*, 20(1):1–9.

Alistair EW Johnson, Tom J Pollard, Lu Shen, H Lehman Li-Wei, Mengling Feng, Mohammad Ghassemi, Benjamin Moody, Peter Szolovits, Leo Anthony Celi, and Roger G Mark. 2016. Mimic-iii, a freely accessible critical care database. *Scientific data*, 3(1):1–9.

Gavin Kerrigan, Dylan Slack, and Jens Tuyls. 2020. Differentially private language models benefit from public pre-training. In *Proceedings of the Second Workshop on Privacy in NLP*, pages 39–45.

Diederik P Kingma and Jimmy Ba. 2015. Adam: A method for stochastic optimization. In *ICLR (Poster)*.

Aleksandra Korolova, Krishnaram Kenthapadi, Nina Mishra, and Alexandros Ntoulas. 2009. Releasing search queries and clicks privately. In *WWW*, pages 171–180. ACM.

Jinhyuk Lee, Wonjin Yoon, Sungdong Kim, Donghyeon Kim, Sunkyu Kim, Chan Ho So, and Jaewoo Kang. 2020. Biobert: a pre-trained biomedical language representation model for biomedical text mining. *Bioinformatics*, 36(4):1234–1240.

H Brendan McMahan, Daniel Ramage, Kunal Talwar, and Li Zhang. 2018. Learning differentially private recurrent language models. In *International Conference on Learning Representations*.

Ilya Mironov. 2017. Rényi differential privacy. In *2017 IEEE 30th Computer Security Foundations Symposium (CSF)*, pages 263–275. IEEE.

Ilya Mironov, Kunal Talwar, and Li Zhang. 2019. Renyi differential privacy of the sampled gaussian mechanism. *arXiv preprint arXiv:1908.10530*.

Daniel Preoţiuc-Pietro, Vasileios Lampos, and Nikolaos Aletras. 2015. An analysis of the user occupational class through twitter content. In *Proceedings of the 53rd Annual Meeting of the Association for Computational Linguistics and the 7th International Joint Conference on Natural Language Processing (Volume 1: Long Papers)*, pages 1754–1764.

Sara Rosenthal and Kathleen McKeown. 2011. Age prediction in blogs: A study of style, content, and online behavior in pre-and post-social media generations. In *Proceedings of the 49th Annual Meeting of the Association for Computational Linguistics: Human Language Technologies*, pages 763–772.

Congzheng Song and Ananth Raghunathan. 2020. Information leakage in embedding models. In *Proceedings of the 2020 ACM SIGSAC Conference on Computer and Communications Security*, pages 377–390.

Shuang Song, Kamalika Chaudhuri, and Anand D Sarwate. 2013. Stochastic gradient descent with differentially private updates. In *2013 IEEE Global Conference on Signal and Information Processing*, pages 245–248. IEEE.

Özlem Uzuner, Brett R South, Shuying Shen, and Scott L DuVall. 2011. 2010 i2b2/va challenge on concepts, assertions, and relations in clinical text. *Journal of the American Medical Informatics Association*, 18(5):552–556.

Y. Wu, M. Schuster, Z. Chen, Q.V. Le, M. Norouzi, W. Macherey, M. Krikun, Y. Cao, Q. Gao, K. Macherey, and J. Klingner. 2016. Google's neural machine translation system: Bridging the gap between human and machine translation. *arXiv preprint arXiv:1609.08144*.

Yukun Zhu, Ryan Kiros, Richard S Zemel, Ruslan Salakhutdinov, Raquel Urtasun, Antonio Torralba, and Sanja Fidler. 2015. Aligning books and movies: Towards story-like visual explanations by watching movies and reading books. In *ICCV*.

An Investigation towards Differentially Private Sequence Tagging in a Federated Framework

Abhik Jana[1] and **Chris Biemann**[1]

[1] Language Technology Group, Dept. of Informatics, Universität Hamburg, Germany
jana@informatik.uni-hamburg.de, biemann@informatik.uni-hamburg.de

Abstract

To build machine learning-based applications for sensitive domains like medical, legal, etc. where the digitized text contains private information, anonymization of text is required for preserving privacy. Sequence tagging, e.g. as used for Named Entity Recognition (NER), can help to detect private information. However, to train sequence tagging models, a sufficient amount of labeled data are required but for privacy-sensitive domains, such labeled data also can not be shared directly. In this paper, we investigate the applicability of a privacy-preserving framework for sequence tagging tasks, specifically NER. Hence, we analyze a framework for the NER task, which incorporates two levels of privacy protection. Firstly, we deploy a federated learning (FL) framework where the labeled data are neither shared with the centralized server nor with the peer clients. Secondly, we apply differential privacy (DP) while the models are being trained in each client instance. While both privacy measures are suitable for privacy-aware models, their combination results in unstable models. To our knowledge, this is the first study of its kind on privacy-aware sequence tagging models.

1 Introduction

The emergence of substantial amounts of digitized unstructured text gives rise to train machine learning models for various downstream applications. But for sensitive domains like medical, legal, etc., the text documents contain private sensitive information, which is supposed to be anonymized for preserving privacy. The first step for anonymizing text is to detect the span of the private information and identify the type of information. Sequence tagging is the kind of task that can help in anonymization. However, to train such a sequence tagging model, a significant amount of labeled data are required. But the labeled data contains – by definition – private sensitive information and are often divided across different data silos. There are legal regulatory policies as well by the US Health Insurance Portability and Accountability Act (HIPAA)[1] and EU General Data Protection Regulation (GDPR) (Agencia-Espanola-Proteccion-Datos, 2019), which restricts such sensitive data access. On the other hand, to train a centralized machine learning model, there is a requirement of aggregating such distributed data in a central server, which can cause privacy breaches. Hence, there is a requirement for a privacy-preserving sequence tagging framework that complies with the data protection policies.

Federated learning (FL) (McMahan et al., 2017) is one such paradigm that provides a framework to train a centralized machine learning model without sharing the distributed data from different data silos. Since the raw data from different data silos are not being shared in this framework, the primary level of privacy is maintained. However, the FL framework is also vulnerable to several inference attacks (Bagdasaryan et al., 2020; Bonawitz et al., 2017; Geyer et al., 2017) in some scenarios. To mitigate such inference attacks, differential privacy (Dwork et al., 2006) was developed, which comes with a theoretically guaranteed measurement of privacy. There have been many recent research works on deploying the FL framework in several applications like image classification (Wang et al., 2019), emotion detection (Chhikara et al., 2021), anonymization (Choudhury et al., 2020), robotics (Imteaj and Amini, 2020), etc. and also in medical domain (Rajendran et al., 2021; Kerkouche et al., 2021; Choudhury et al., 2019; Ge et al., 2020). Researchers also investigated the scope of the differentially private algorithm in several applications (Zhao et al., 2020; Koda et al., 2020; Hu et al., 2020; Chen et al., 2018). However, for sequence

[1] https://www.hhs.gov/hipaa/for-professionals/privacy/special-topics/de-identification/index.html

Proceedings of the 58th Annual Meeting of the Association for Computational Linguistics, pages 30–35
July 5–10, 2020. ©2020 Association for Computational Linguistics
https://doi.org/10.26615/978-954-452-056-4_004

tagging tasks, the applicability of the FL framework along with differential privacy (DP) is yet to be explored. For our study, we focus on one such sequence tagging task, namely named entity recognition (NER). We argue that this is quite close to a sequence-tagging based anonymization task and it allows us to study the effects of privatization measures in the task performance.

In this paper, we prepare an FL framework following the FederatedAveraging (McMahan et al., 2017) approach and deploy a differentially private stochastic gradient descent (Abadi et al., 2016) optimizer while training to obtain differential privacy for the NER task. As base NER models, we consider two variants of one of the state-of-the-art approaches for sequence labeling, that uses the LSTM variant (Hochreiter and Schmidhuber, 1997) of bidirectional recurrent neural networks (BiLSTMs). Note that the aim of our work is not to produce a state-of-the-art performance for NER tasks. Rather, our focus is to analyze how the performance of NER models varies in a differentially private federated learning framework. Therefore, we do a comprehensive analysis using CoNLL 2003 English NER dataset and investigate the effect of different levels of privacy on the performance of NER models.

2 Methodology

As we deal with the named entity recognition (NER) task, we attempt with two variations of BiLSTM based models. In one variant we keep TimeDistributed Dense layer (TDDL) as the final layer with activation function – 'softmax' and in another variant, we keep the conditional random field (CRF) (Huang et al., 2015) as the final layer. In a nutshell, both the variants have three layers: Input embedding layer, Bidirectional LSTM layer, and either TDDL or CRF as the final layer. We refer to those model variants 'BI-LSTM-TDDL' and 'BI-LSTM-CRF' respectively for our study. Next, we will discuss the two privacy mechanisms: Federated Learning and Differential Privacy.

Federated Learning: The objective of the Federated Learning framework is to train a centralized model from data distributed across multiple client data silos, eliminating the need for raw data sharing. We adapt the well-accepted FederatedAveraging algorithm proposed by McMahan et al. (2017). As per the process, first, a global model from the server site is shared across n client sites. Next, each client site trains the model based on its local data. After the training is complete, the parameter updates of the local models are then subsequently sent to the central aggregation server. Next, the central server computes the average of all the model parameters over n clients and updates the global model accordingly. The whole process continues for specified number of rounds (t) and in each round a random set of m clients ($m <= n$) participate. For this study, in each round we allow all the n client sites to participate in the process.

Differential Privacy: The objective of differential privacy is to provide a strong criterion for privacy preservation of distributed data processing systems. This is a widely used privacy-preserving mechanism due to its strong information-theoretic guarantees (Dwork and Roth, 2014), algorithmic simplicity, and relatively small systems overhead. By definition, any randomized algorithm $A(D)$ satisfies ϵ - differential privacy if for all datasets D and D', that differ by a single record, and for all sets $S \in R$, where R is the range of A,

$$Pr[A(D) \in S] \leq e^{\epsilon} Pr[A(D') \in S]$$

where ϵ, is a non-negative number. ϵ measures the strength of the privacy guarantee of the algorithm. It gives a bound on how much the probability of particular model output can vary by including (or removing) a single training example. The lower the value of ϵ, the higher the privacy. There are several methods for incorporating differential privacy in an algorithm. For this study, we adopt the approach that relies on Differentially Private Stochastic Gradient Descent (DP-SGD) optimizer proposed by Abadi et al. (2016). As per this approach, after sampling a micro-batch of training points we need to compute the loss and gradient of the loss. Thereafter, we need to clip gradients, per the training example included in the micro-batch. Next, we need to add random noise to the clipped gradients and multiply these clipped and noised gradients by the learning rate and apply the product to update model parameters.

3 Experiments and Discussions

Since the objective of our work is to investigate the effect of federated learning (**FL**) framework and differential privacy (**DP**) on the state-of-the-art NER model, we design our analysis in four different phases. First, we observe the basic NER model performance without using FL as well as DP. In the second phase, we incorporate DP in the optimizer of the NER model and analyze its behavior. Third, we analyze the performance of the NER model in an FL framework, but none of the optimizers of the clients are DP enabled. In the fourth phase, we investigate the performance of the NER model by deploying the FL framework and incorporating DP into the client-side optimizers. For our analysis, we use CoNLL 2003 English NER dataset, having a training set size of 14987, validation set size of 3466, and test set size of 3684. Each token in the dataset is tagged with other (O) or one of the four entity types: Person (PER), Location (LOC), Organization (ORG), Miscellaneous (MISC). Considering the BIO2 annotation standard, the number of possible labels for each token is 9.

Model	Precision	Recall	F-measure
BI-LSTM-TDDL	0.916	0.922	0.916
BI-LSTM-CRF	0.892	0.862	0.864

Table 1: Performance of Basic NER models.

Noise-multiplier	0.5	1	5	10	50
ϵ	3.73	0.688	0.05	0.024	0.022
BI-LSTM-TDDL					
Precision	0.915	0.911	0.917	0.914	0.911
Recall	0.919	0.911	0.924	0.912	0.913
F-measure	0.913	0.906	0.916	0.908	0.908
BI-LSTM-CRF					
Precision	0.869	0.727	0.825	0.889	0.839
Recall	0.847	0.809	0.786	0.834	0.816
F-measure	0.839	0.75	0.802	0.840	0.815

Table 2: Performance of NER models after incorporating ϵ differentially Private SGD.

$(n) \rightarrow$	2	5	10	15	20
Precision	0.905	0.881	0.824	0.792	0.786
Recall	0.903	0.885	0.830	0.814	0.803
F-measure	0.897	0.874	0.805	0.784	0.766

Table 3: Performance of BI-LSTM-TDDL model in the FL setup, with increasing number of clients (n).

Training Data	Precision mean	Precision sd	Recall mean	Recall sd	F-measure mean	F-measure sd
20 %	0.756	0.002	0.798	0.000	0.762	0.000
40 %	0.814	0.006	0.824	0.001	0.797	0.001
60 %	0.832	0.001	0.842	0.000	0.820	0.000
80 %	0.845	0.009	0.854	0.000	0.835	0.001
100 %	0.861	0.005	0.863	0.000	0.846	0.001

Table 4: Performance of BI-LSTM-TDDL model in the FL setup, with increasing % of training data in each client. Number of clients = 5. Mean and standard deviation (sd) are computed over 5 different simulations.

Without DP, Without FL: We experiment with two different NER models described in Section 2[2]. The vector embeddings used is GloVe (trained on Common Crawl corpus) from spaCy library[3], the dimension of which is 300. The performance of these two models (BI-LSTM-TDDL, BI-LSTM-CRF) are presented in Table 1. Note that, since our objective is not to produce a state-of-the-art performance for NER tasks, we do not attempt to tune the hyper-parameters to obtain the best possible performance. However, the F-measure obtained by BI-LSTM-TDDL is comparable to the state-of-the-art (Akbik et al., 2018) F-measure of 0.9309. On the other hand, we put our effort into analyzing the behavior of these NER models' performance in privacy preserving framework.

With DP, Without FL: Next, we incorporate a Differentially Private Stochastic gradient descent (DP-SGD) optimizer for training[4]. The performance of both the models with varying noise-multiplier (a hyperparameter to add noise) are presented in Table 2. Note that, by increasing the value of noise-multiplier we add more privacy (lower ϵ) to the NER models. We observe, even if the privacy increases, the BI-LSTM-TDDL model produces stable performance and does not deteriorate much compared to its performance while DP is not present. On the other hand, using DP-SGD, BI-LSTM-CRF architecture performs poorly and fluctuates significantly. We observe a negative signal towards incorporating DP, where model architecture has CRF in the final layer, for tasks like NER. Finding out the reason behind such behavior of CRF-based model and mitigating the problem would be immediate future work. However, for the next two phases of analysis, we continue only with the robust BI-LSTM-TDDL model architecture.

$(n) \rightarrow$	2	5	10	15	20
Precision	0.835	0.804	0.752	0.731	0.740
Recall	0.867	0.845	0.815	0.810	0.801
F-measure	0.834	0.810	0.772	0.763	0.758

Table 5: Performance of BI-LSTM-TDDL model in the FL setup along with DP, with increasing number of clients (n). Noise multiplier = 1, $\epsilon = 0.688$

Without DP, With FL: Next, we analyze the FL setup for NER, where we have one centralized server and n number of the client sites. The training and validation data are divided equally among all the clients. We analyze the framework in two ways. First, we observe the performance variation of the aggregated model on test data with the number of clients, which is presented in Table 3. The

[2]The hyperparameter settings to train those models are as follows: epochs- 10, batch size - 32, learning rate - 0.15, optimizer - Stochastic gradient descent (SGD)

[3]https://spacy.io/models/en#en_core_web_lg

[4]we use Tensorflow Privacy library https://github.com/tensorflow/privacy/blob/master/tensorflow_privacy. The hyperparameter settings: micro-batch size - 1, normalization clip - 1.5

Training Data	Precision		Recall		F-measure	
	mean	sd	mean	sd	mean	sd
20 %	0.767	0.008	0.745	0.033	0.744	0.013
40 %	0.773	0.006	0.738	0.029	0.744	0.013
60 %	0.707	0.102	0.123	0.063	0.171	0.104
80 %	0.812	0.052	0.113	0.172	0.106	0.231
100 %	0.585	0.556	0.137	0.228	0.123	0.269

Table 6: Performance of BI-LSTM-TDDL model in the FL setup along with DP, with increasing % of training data used in each client. Mean and standard deviation (sd) are computed over 5 different simulation. Number of clients = 5, Noise multiplier = 1, $\epsilon = 0.688$.

results are reported only after one communication round, i.e. all the client models are trained with their respective training data (full) and the client models' parameters are transferred to the central server once for aggregation. From the result in Table 3, we see with the increasing number of clients the performance of the centralized NER model decreases. Given that the number of the training sample is constant and those are divided among the clients equally, the observed performance fits our intuitions. As the number of clients increases, the amount of training data per client decreases, and the client models are trained with a smaller amount of training data[5]. Secondly, we observe how the central model behaves if model parameters are shared from clients after training the client models with $x\%$ of the local training data. For our study we keep $x = 10$, which implies client model aggregation and global model update cycle is being executed after each pass of model training with 10 % of local data on the client-side. Since the $x\%$ of data is picked randomly, we simulate independently for 5 times and report the mean and standard deviation (sd) of all metrics. From the results presented in Table 4, we observe that even in such an incremental training scenario we achieve an F-measure of 0.846 with 100% training data, which is comparable to the non-incremental version of training (0.874 as per Table 3). The FL setup for the NER model looks promising in the incremental approach as well, making it suitable even for the scenario while on the client-side a large amount of training data is not available at once.

With DP, With FL: We attempt two different analyses following the same experimental setup as 'Without DP, With FL', but during client-side training, we use DP-SGD instead of SGD as the optimizer. In Table 5, we see that the trend of decreasing F-measure with the increasing number of clients, which is the same as the non-private performance. Note that, when we incorporate DP in FL setup it reduces the F-measure about 1-6 %. The result for the second type of analysis is presented in Table 6. We note that with increasing percentage (%) of training data, the F-measure does not improve, and after some point (60 %) the F-measure drops significantly. DP does not seem promising for incremental setup, while in each phase the training data used is sufficiently small. Note that, in each phase, only $x = 10\%$ training data (approx. 300 data points) is being used for training.

4 Conclusion

In this work, we presented an analysis of the behavior of one sequence tagging task namely NER in a federated learning framework along with differential privacy, which is the first-ever attempt of its kind. From the investigation, we observed that with DP-SGD optimizer, the performance of CRF based model tends to decrease significantly in our current experimental setup. In the federated framework, we observed that with the increase of the number of clients with smaller training data, the performance of aggregated models decrease significantly, whereas the performance shoots up when client models are trained in an incremental approach and the incremental models are communicated to the server after each training phase. On the other hand, when a DP-SGD optimizer is deployed in each client training phase, even the incremental training policy works only till 60% of the training data is used and thereafter performance drops. Immediate future work would be to find out the root cause of such a phenomenon and mitigate it, as a combination of privacy measures would be very much desired in privacy-aware application scenarios.

To extend this study, we plan to explore several other NER datasets (even low-resource datasets) to find out more general behavior. Hyper-parameter tuning is another direction of our future work to find out the best performance for each set-up. The broader goal is to build a differentially private federated framework for sequence tagging tasks with compromising performance as little as possible.

Acknowledgements

This research was funded by the German Federal Ministry of Education and Research (BMBF) as part of the HILANO project, ID 01IS18085C.

[5]The hyperparameter settings for training client model: epochs - 10, batch size - 32, learning rate - 0.15, optimizer - Stochastic gradient descent (SGD).

References

Martin Abadi, Andy Chu, Ian Goodfellow, H Brendan McMahan, Ilya Mironov, Kunal Talwar, and Li Zhang. 2016. Deep learning with differential privacy. In *Proceedings of the 2016 ACM SIGSAC conference on computer and communications security*, pages 308–318, Vienna, Austria.

Agencia-Espanola-Proteccion-Datos. 2019. K-anonymity as a privacy measure. `https://www.aepd.es/sites/default/files/2019-09/nota-tecnica-kanonimidad-en.pdf`.

Alan Akbik, Duncan Blythe, and Roland Vollgraf. 2018. Contextual string embeddings for sequence labeling. In *Proceedings of the 27th international conference on computational linguistics*, pages 1638–1649, Santa Fe, New Mexico, USA.

Eugene Bagdasaryan, Andreas Veit, Yiqing Hua, Deborah Estrin, and Vitaly Shmatikov. 2020. How to backdoor federated learning. In *International Conference on Artificial Intelligence and Statistics*, pages 2938–2948, Palermo, Sicily, Italy.

Keith Bonawitz, Vladimir Ivanov, Ben Kreuter, Antonio Marcedone, H Brendan McMahan, Sarvar Patel, Daniel Ramage, Aaron Segal, and Karn Seth. 2017. Practical secure aggregation for privacy-preserving machine learning. In *proceedings of the 2017 ACM SIGSAC Conference on Computer and Communications Security*, pages 1175–1191, Dallas, Texas, USA.

Qingrong Chen, Chong Xiang, Minhui Xue, Bo Li, Nikita Borisov, Dali Kaarfar, and Haojin Zhu. 2018. Differentially private data generative models. *arXiv preprint arXiv:1812.02274*.

Prateek Chhikara, Prabhjot Singh, Rajkumar Tekchandani, Neeraj Kumar, and Mohsen Guizani. 2021. Federated learning meets human emotions: A decentralized framework for human–computer interaction for iot applications. *IEEE Internet of Things Journal*, 8(8):6949–6962.

Olivia Choudhury, Aris Gkoulalas-Divanis, Theodoros Salonidis, Issa Sylla, Yoonyoung Park, Grace Hsu, and Amar Das. 2019. Differential privacy-enabled federated learning for sensitive health data. *arXiv preprint arXiv:1910.02578*.

Olivia Choudhury, Aris Gkoulalas-Divanis, Theodoros Salonidis, Issa Sylla, Yoonyoung Park, Grace Hsu, and Amar Das. 2020. Anonymizing data for privacy-preserving federated learning. *arXiv preprint arXiv:2002.09096*.

Cynthia Dwork, Krishnaram Kenthapadi, Frank McSherry, Ilya Mironov, and Moni Naor. 2006. Our data, ourselves: Privacy via distributed noise generation. In *Annual International Conference on the Theory and Applications of Cryptographic Techniques*, pages 486–503, Saint Petersburg, Russia.

Cynthia Dwork and Aaron Roth. 2014. The algorithmic foundations of differential privacy. *Foundations and Trends in Theoretical Computer Science*, 9(3-4):211–407.

Suyu Ge, Fangzhao Wu, Chuhan Wu, Tao Qi, Yongfeng Huang, and Xing Xie. 2020. Fedner: Privacy-preserving medical named entity recognition with federated learning. *arXiv preprint arXiv:2003.09288*.

Robin C Geyer, Tassilo Klein, and Moin Nabi. 2017. Differentially private federated learning: A client level perspective. *arXiv preprint arXiv:1712.07557*.

Sepp Hochreiter and Jürgen Schmidhuber. 1997. Long short-term memory. *Neural computation*, 9(8):1735–1780.

Rui Hu, Yuanxiong Guo, E Paul Ratazzi, and Yanmin Gong. 2020. Differentially private federated learning for resource-constrained internet of things. *arXiv preprint arXiv:2003.12705*.

Zhiheng Huang, Wei Xu, and Kai Yu. 2015. Bidirectional LSTM-CRF models for sequence tagging. *arXiv preprint arXiv:1508.01991*.

Ahmed Imteaj and M Hadi Amini. 2020. Fedar: Activity and resource-aware federated learning model for distributed mobile robots. *arXiv preprint arXiv:2101.03705*.

Raouf Kerkouche, Gergely Acs, Claude Castelluccia, and Pierre Genevès. 2021. Privacy-preserving and bandwidth-efficient federated learning: An application to in-hospital mortality prediction. In *ACM Conference on Health, Inference, and Learning*, page 25–35, Virtual Event, USA.

Yusuke Koda, Koji Yamamoto, Takayuki Nishio, and Masahiro Morikura. 2020. Differentially private aircomp federated learning with power adaptation harnessing receiver noise. *arXiv preprint arXiv:2004.06337*.

Brendan McMahan, Eider Moore, Daniel Ramage, Seth Hampson, and Blaise Aguera y Arcas. 2017. Communication-efficient learning of deep networks from decentralized data. In *Proceedings of the 20th International Conference on Artificial Intelligence and Statistics*, pages 1273–1282, Fort Lauderdale, Florida, USA.

Suraj Rajendran, Jihad S Obeid, Hamidullah Binol, Ralph D Agostino Jr, Kristie Foley, Wei Zhang, Philip Austin, Joey Brakefield, Metin N Gurcan, and Umit Topaloglu. 2021. Cloud-based federated learning implementation across medical centers. *JCO clinical cancer informatics*, 5:1–11.

Shiqiang Wang, Tiffany Tuor, Theodoros Salonidis, Kin K Leung, Christian Makaya, Ting He, and Kevin Chan. 2019. Adaptive federated learning in resource constrained edge computing systems. *IEEE Journal on Selected Areas in Communications*, 37(6):1205–1221.

Yang Zhao, Jun Zhao, Mengmeng Yang, Teng Wang, Ning Wang, Lingjuan Lyu, Dusit Niyato, and Kwok-Yan Lam. 2020. Local differential privacy based federated learning for internet of things. *IEEE Internet of Things Journal*, Early Access.

A Privacy-Preserving Approach to Extraction of Personal Information through Automatic Annotation and Federated Learning

Rajitha Hathurusinghe[1]*, **Isar Nejadgholi**[2]*, **Miodrag Bolic**[3]
[1,2,3]University of Ottawa, Ottawa, Canada
[2]National Research Council Canada, Ottawa, Canada
[1,3]{rhath050,Miodrag.Bolic}@uottawa.ca
[2]isar.nejadgholi@nrc-cnrc.gc.ca

Abstract

We curated WikiPII, an automatically labeled dataset composed of Wikipedia biography pages, annotated for personal information extraction. Although automatic annotation can lead to a high degree of label noise, it is an inexpensive process and can generate large volumes of annotated documents. We trained a BERT-based NER model with WikiPII and showed that with an adequately large training dataset, the model can significantly decrease the cost of manual information extraction, despite the high level of label noise. In a similar approach, organizations can leverage text mining techniques to create customized annotated datasets from their historical data without sharing the raw data for human annotation. Also, we explore collaborative training of NER models through federated learning when the annotation is noisy. Our results suggest that depending on the level of trust to the ML operator and the volume of the available data, distributed training can be an effective way of training a personal information identifier in a privacy-preserved manner. Research material is available at `https://github.com/ratmcu/wikipiifed`.

1 Introduction

Extraction of Personally Identifiable Information (PII) from unstructured text is a crucial task in many industries such as healthcare (e.g (Li and Qin, 2017; Kushida et al., 2012)) legal documents (Oksanen et al., 2019), mining of user-generated data (Mosallanezhad et al., 2019) and publication process (Aura et al., 2006). PII is a laborious task, often necessary for de-identification purposes, among other applications. For example, the extracted information can be used for indexing of documents, categorization and other applications. Identification of PII elements is a laborious task that can be automated by deploying Named Entity Recognition (NER) models (Hassan et al., 2018; Graliński et al., 2009). We formulate PII recognition as a NER task that extracts predefined PII entities. Our goal is to develop NER models to decrease this task's cost by preprocessing documents before manual information extraction.

Supervised machine learning approaches such as Conditional Random Field (CRF) models, Support vector machines, and extensive feature engineering based on lexical and phrase embeddings have been used to train NER systems (Luo et al., 2015; Passos et al., 2014; Retinov and Roth, 2009). With improvements of deep learning models, recurrent neural networks and specially LSTM models became the default model for training NER systems (Chiu and Nichols, 2016). Recently, a combination of pre-trained transformer-based language models and linear or recurrent prediction layers achieved the state-of-the-art in most NER tasks (Dai et al., 2019; Fraser et al., 2019).

Training a NER model for extraction of PII demands a massive corpus of text, rich in personal information, which raises privacy concerns in the process of data annotation and model training. Although NER models achieve high performance in cross-validation settings, the generalization of off-the-shelf models remains poor (Fu et al., 2020). For training a robust PII recognizer, a customized domain-specific annotated dataset is needed (Chen et al., 2015). In this work, our goal is to bring privacy to the front line of designing a PII extractor from dataset creation to model training.

We consider a scenario where an institution intends to build an assistant tool to decrease the cost of manual PII extraction. We assume that the institution has accumulated documents alongside their corresponding PII fields over the years, but PII elements are not necessarily marked within the text. This is the typical case for many institutions (such as hospitals and banks), which have manually extracted PII elements for years. For example, a hospital has access to patients' names and ages for every specific health record. However, the locations of occurrences of name and age within the documents are unknown. Also, the name and age can

* Equal contribution.

Proceedings of the 58th Annual Meeting of the Association for Computational Linguistics, pages 36–45
July 5–10, 2020. ©2020 Association for Computational Linguistics
https://doi.org/10.26615/978-954-452-056-4_005

come in various forms and lengths when mentioned in free text. To build a useful training dataset for a PII recognizer, the hospital needs to mark phrases related to name and age in the free text through text mining. However, sharing this data for annotation and training involves privacy considerations. We consider the following steps to ensure our process is compliant with the privacy of data subjects.

- Annotating the free text programmatically without the need for sharing the data for human annotation.
- Distributed storing of annotated documents so that the data can be kept in authorized locations.
- Remote training of the PII extraction model without the need for sharing annotated documents with machine learning practitioners.

To conduct a reproducible research, we show the feasibility of the proposed approach on a dataset collected from Wikipedia and share the created dataset and results with research community. Our contributions are as following:

- We create and release an automatically labeled dataset comprised of 77703 sentences from Wikipedia biography pages annotated for 5 classes of personal information.
- We develop a method for remote training of a transformer-based model on distributed datasets, using PySyft platform.
- We explore the impact of label noise and dataset size on the performance of remotely trained NER models.

2 WikiPII Dataset

Our goal is to create and annotate a customized textual dataset for training a PII extractor (the scenario described in Section 1). Approaches like snorkel (Ratner et al., 2017) had been embracing noise of automatic annotations and compensated the noise by adding to the volume of inexpensive data. We took the same approach for annotating Wikipedia pages and benefited from the fact that a version of entities was available in the infobox. We used the infobox to generate noisy and inexpensive data annotations, whereas snorkel uses multiple noisy parallel annotation functions and weak-supervision from alternative sources.

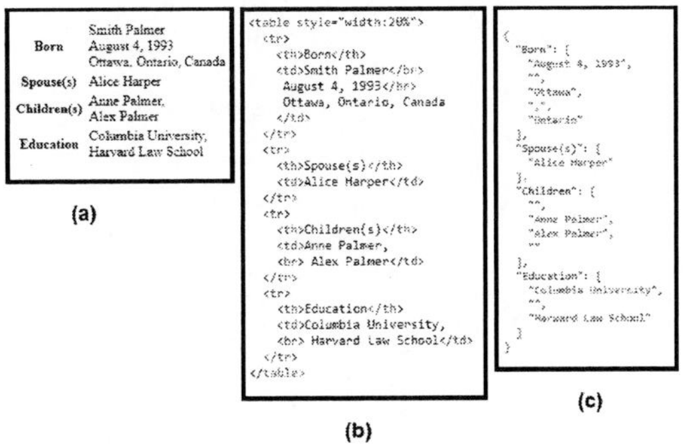

Figure 1: Infobox a) viewed on web page, b) in HTML format, c) converted to a dictionary

We collected our data from Wikipedia biography pages because 1) they are rich in terms of PII, 2) with the infobox available on each page, they comply with our assumption of having access to extracted PII, 3) they are publicly available and can be shared and used as a benchmark for research purposes. Similar automated annotation tasks such as Nothman et al. (2013) utilized a broader set of Wikipedia pages and contain general CoNLL style (Sang and De Meulder, 2003) (location, organization, person, miscellaneous) classes of entities and does not focus on granular personal information as ours. We refer to this dataset as WikiPII and release this data for further research.

2.1 Data Collection

We scraped our raw textual data from biography page entries of living people in Wikipedia (about 900K pages). For programmatic annotation of each page's textual body, we first read the HTML-coded infobox and converted it to a PII element dictionary, using the BeautifulSoup[1] package. An example of this conversion is demonstrated in Figure 1.

Next, we normalized the similar entity types to acquire consistent entity types across all pages. For example, the spouse's name can come under the titles' Spouse',' Spouse(s)' and' Spouses', which are all normalized to the 'SP' tag. After normalization, we manually inspected the entities and chose the ones with high coverage in the dataset. At last, we decided to include BD (date of birth), PR (names of parents), SP (names of spouse(s)), CH (names of children) and ED (terms of education institutes attended). Our final tags and their corresponding

[1] https://www.crummy.com/software/BeautifulSoup/bs4/doc/

infobox entries are shown in Table 1 [2].

Tag	Corresponding entries in infobox
Birth Date (BD)	'Born', 'Born:'
Parents (PR)	'Parent', 'Parent(s)', 'Parents', 'Father', 'Father's name', 'Mother', 'Mother's name
Spouses (SP)	'Spouse', 'Spouse(s)', 'Spouses'
Children (CH)	'Children'
Education (ED)	'Education', 'High school', 'High school:', 'Law School', 'School', 'Schools', 'College', 'College(s)', 'Colleges', 'Alma mater','Almat mater'

Table 1: Tags included in our dataset and corresponding entities in infobox.

2.2 Labeling of Entities in Text

Once the PII was extracted from the infobox, we had to locate them in the text and generate a tag for each word to create an annotated dataset. This step's main challenge is that the mentions of entities in the text might be variations of the ones extracted from the infobox.

We parsed the textual body into sentences and removed citation brackets and numerals using regular expressions. For each tag shown in Table 1, we develop a function that takes the extracted phrase from infobox and locates that phrase within the free text. We combine two different methods of matching to get a more accurate match. Our entities are subcategories of places, organizations, persons and dates, which SpaCy already covers. We leveraged the part-of-speech and named entity recognition capabilities of the SpaCy[3] package to find noun chunks, person names, locations, organizations and dates. Then, depending on the type of the entity, we choose a subset of extracted phrases and use fuzzy string matching[4] to find the closest phrase to our target phrase. For example, for the tag, ED (education), we extract all the organization names by SpaCy. We then use fuzzy matching to find the variations of the education institute pulled from the infobox.

[2]We first extracted birthplace from the infobox, but places are mentioned in several formats such as town, province, country, etc. We omit this entity in the final tagging.

[3]We used the *en_core_web_lg* pipeline from `https://spacy.io/usage/facts-figures#benchmarks`, which is highly accurate in NER task and optimized in terms of speed.

[4]We utilized the implementation published at `https://github.com/axiak/fuzzyset/` for fuzzy matching.

We used the BIO scheme for tagging of words. NER is a sequence to sequence learning task that predicts a label for each word, specifying whether the word is within or outside an entity and the entities' type. In the BIO format, the tags 'B_', 'I_', and 'O_' mark the beginning, inside and outside of an entity, respectively. For example, 'B_CH' specifies the beginning of a phrase tagged as 'Children'. The combination of these tags specifies the boundary and tag of the extracted entity. Therefore, error analysis of an NER task is based on errors in tag and boundary detection. These error are reflected in the evaluation metrics described in Section 3.

2.3 Manual Annotation

To evaluate the quality of the programmatic annotation, we manually annotated a subset of the pages. We selected pages that include highest numbers of entities and made sure that the manually annotated dataset contains 50 to 100 mentions of each class. Manual annotation is done by re-annotating the entities already found by the automated annotator. A human annotator can choose to confirm, reject or correct the labels created by the automatic annotation. We designed a user interface for the manual annotation where the annotator had access to the infobox elements and their corresponding tags. An example of the designed annotator user interface is shown in Figure 2.

Figure 3 shows examples of common mistakes in the automatic annotation. Entities extracted from the infobox are shown in the left column. The yellow entities are missed by automated annotation and corrected by the human annotator. These entities are missed because they are missing from the infobox. Also, since the automatic annotation does not consider the context, it cannot resolve ambiguities. In the example of Figure 3 'Troy' is a city name but is tagged as CH (children) since it appears as a child name in the infobox. Also, 'Harvard University', which is tagged as an education institute, is not a PII element for the main subject of the page but an affiliation of someone else. In manual annotation, 'Troy' and 'Harvard University' will be corrected and not tagged as an entity.

2.4 Statistics of WikiPII dataset

Our data source contains over 900K entries. Our annotation method could only use a little over 23K entries due to formatting changes in the Wikipedia pages where infobox is not available. We filtered the sentences that do not include any of our target

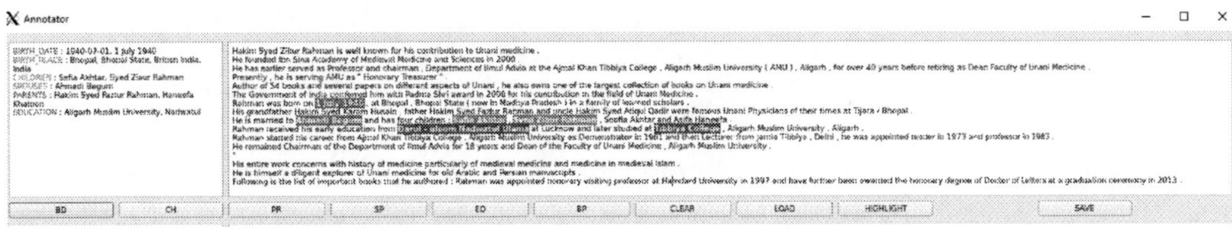

Figure 2: Annotator UI for manual annotation.

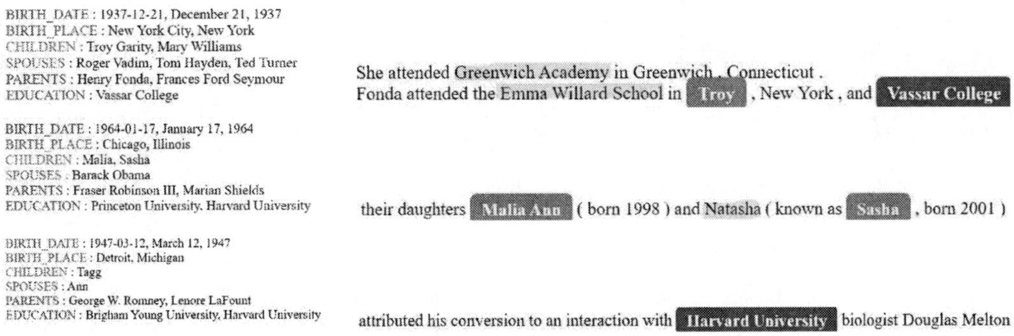

Figure 3: Examples of mistakes in automated annotation.

entities. The dataset contains a large number of PII instances belonging to over 23K individuals worldwide belonging to 5 classes. Separate splits of the created dataset and numbers of entities contained are presented in Table 2.

3 Evaluation of PII extraction

Averaged F-score is a common metric to evaluate a NER system. However, the definition of a True Positive and a True Negative prediction is not always trivial. Since identifying an entity involves finding both the span and type of the entity, some of the system's predictions can be partially correct. Multiple evaluation schemes have been developed. Shared tasks such as IREX (Sekine and Isahara, 1999), and CoNLL (Sang and De Meulder, 2003) only gave credit to the exacted entities with the exact type and boundary matches. Other works have adopted *type matching* or *partial matching* evaluation schemes, which reward partially correct entity extractions (Tsai et al., 2006; Chinchor and Sundheim, 1993; Segura Bedmar et al., 2013). Learning-based evaluation methods are developed to predict the user experience in specific tasks (Nejadgholi et al., 2020).

PII extraction is a sensitive task, and a fully automatic system cannot be reliable. Instead, the output of such systems are used to augment the performance of manual PII extraction. In practice, when a human is in the loop, partial matching can reduce the manual effort of PII extraction. We adopted the metrics introduced by the MUC-5 task (Chinchor and Sundheim, 1993), and SemEval-13 task 9 (Segura Bedmar et al., 2013) and implemented the following evaluation metrics ordered in terms of strictness:

- **Strict Matching:** rewards a prediction only if boundary and type of entity match with gold standard label. This metric evaluates the system in a fully automated PII extraction setting.
- **Exact Boundary:** rewards a prediction if the boundary of extracted entity matches the gold standard labeling. This metric evaluates the system where the human annotator relies on boundaries predicted by the system and only corrects the label if necessary.
- **Type Matching:** rewards the strict matches and partially ($\times 0.5$) rewards the extracted entities where the type is correct and boundary overlaps with the gold standard. This metric evaluates the system where the human annotator relies on types predicted by the system and only corrects the boundary if necessary.
- **Partial Boundary:** rewards strict matches and partially ($\times 0.5$) rewards where the boundary overlaps with the gold standard label regardless of type. This metric evaluates the

Data split / annotation method	Pages	Sentences	BD	PR	SP	CH	ED
training/automatic	20039	77703	16883	6326	25163	10824	24365
validation/automatic	2744	12267	2512	1509	3844	1846	3831
test/automatic	307	2051	303	331	609	604	534
test/manual	91	320	76	50	80	62	92

Table 2: Count of pages, sentences which contain at least one of the target entities and number of mentions per each class of entities for different splits of the WikiPII dataset.

Predicted Entity	strict	exact	type	partial	implication in PII extraction
$_{name}$ Adam London.	✓✓	✓✓	✓✓	✓✓	no need for correction.
Adam $_{name}$ London.	✗	✗	✓	✓	boundary should be corrected.
$_{place}$ Adam London.	✗	✓✓	✗	✓	type should be corrected.
Adam $_{place}$ London.	✗	✗	✗	✓	entity is located, boundary and type should be corrected.

Table 3: Examples of predicted entity with respect to various evaluation metrics. ✗indicates no reward, ✓indicates half point reward and ✓✓indicates a full reward.

system where the human annotator relies on the location of predictions and corrects both label and boundary if necessary.

Table 3 shows examples of predicted entities by a PII recognizer with respect to the evaluation metrics and the cost of correction in a human-in-the-loop PII recognition task.

4 PII Extraction model

First, we evaluate the automated annotation compared to the manual annotation. Then we use the automatically annotated train set to train a BERT-based NER model with a fully connected linear layer as the prediction layer. We then evaluate the performance of the trained PII recognizer on both automatically and manually annotated test sets.

4.1 Comparison between Manual and Automatic Annotation

To evaluate the automatic annotation, we take manual annotations as the gold standard and score the corresponding automated annotations with the metrics described in Section 3. Table 4 shows the results of this evaluation. As discussed in Section 3, we used different metrics to evaluate this model based on the real-application scenario. For example, partial metric evaluates the scenario where the model is used to assist the human annotator in locating the entities. We observe that the rule-based annotation tool leads to high levels of noise. With partial evaluation, we conclude that automatic annotation spots about half of the entities correctly, but the boundary and type might not be fully correct. On the other side, the strict metric indicates that about one-third of the entities are perfectly annotated. Also, the type metric is higher than the exact metric, indicating that automatic annotation performs better in predicting types than boundaries. This is expected because of the complexities and subjectivity of boundary identification.

	strict	exact	type	partial
precision	0.31	0.32	0.39	0.46
recall	0.45	0.46	0.57	0.65
F1-score	0.37	0.38	0.47	0.54

Table 4: Evaluation of automated annotation compared to the manual annotation.

4.2 Performance of PII Extraction Model

We fine-tuned a BERT-based NER model with the training split of the automatically annotated WikiPII dataset to build a PII recognizer and tested the trained model with the test split of automatically annotated dataset and the manually annotated test set. We choose a batch size of 128 sentences and a maximum length of 50 tokens and present the results for one epoch of training. The optimum number of epochs varies between 1 and 3 for different datasets, but for the sake of comparison we choose to run all experiments with one epoch. Table 5 shows the results of this experiment.

We observed that despite the high level of noise in the automatically annotated training dataset the trained NER model reaches an acceptable performance. This is due to the large size of the automatically annotated dataset. As Rolnick et al. (2017) showed, deep learning models are robust to label noise when the size of the dataset is adequately large. We observed that the partial metric is

80%, which indicates a significant decrease in manual cost of PII extraction. While these predictions might still need corrections of type and boundary the system can locate most of the entities. From the strict metric, we conclude that half of the PII elements are predicted correctly in label and span and do not need any correction. Comparing of the exact and type metric shows that in most cases the system predicts the label correctly and boundaries need to be corrected.

5 Distributed Training

Modern deep learning models are known as data-hungry algorithms. In the task of PII extraction, sharing data across organizations will lead to more robust models. However, sharing of personal data in a central location involves concerns of privacy. To mitigate the risk of data breaches, we can train machine learning models in a distributed fashion while leaving the data in a location governed by the data owners. In this work, we explore Federated Learning (FL) (Yang et al., 2019) for training a NER model with noisy labelled data. Federated learning involves training statistical models over remote data centers, such as mobile phones or hospitals, while keeping data localized without requiring transfer of the whole dataset to a central location.

To implement FL, we use the PySyft framework, developed by *OpenMined* [5]. This framework is developed in PyTorch and provides the platform for executing tensor operations remotely (Ryffel et al., 2018). PySyft has been developed under the theme *"Answer questions you cannot see"*, to perform machine learning inference with zero knowledge about the specifics of the data.

In this framework, a central entity orchestrates the training scenario. Data is maintained and tagged by its owners at a remote location. At each data location, a worker follows the commands of the central entity. The model is transferred to the remote location, and updates are completed remotely at each training iteration. Subsequently, the final model is updated by averaging weights, averaging remote gradient updates or consecutive updates at each dataset location (Li et al., 2020).

5.1 Federated Training of BERT-based Model

BERT (Bidirectional Encoder Representations from Transformers) is a transformer-based language model pre-trained on a massive corpus of written text. BERT and a series of language models belonging to BERT's family form the backbone of today's deep learning NLP models. The language model generates a vector representation for the input text and passes it on to the downstream task. The pre-trained language model is usually fine-tuned with the task-specific data during task-specific learning. In this work, we only use BERT-based NER model, with a fully connected linear layer as the prediction layer, but the general idea applies to other transformer-based language models.Training and testing splits are the same as the ones used in Section 4.2.

The input to a BERT model contains three tensors: Token type id (specifies single sentence or double sentence use of the model), position ids (specifies the position of the token in the sentence), and input ids (specifies the id of the word in the vocabulary) (Devlin et al., 2018). Except for input ids, all the other inputs are tensors generated dynamically at the training time. The pre-trained tokenizer model generates these inputs to be based on the dimensions of the input sentence batches.

PySyft is designed in a way that abstracts the remote tensor objects by wrapping them around an empty tensor located centrally. Wrapping the tensor is the process of maintaining an empty local tensor object, while executing tensor operations on the remote tensor through the network. This method abstracts the location separation and allows the central worker to operate on tensor objects just as they were situated centrally. One drawback of this wrapping-based abstraction is that the functions such as size querying are operated on the local empty tensor rather than the native real tensor located in the remote worker. For that reason, the PySyft framework cannot query the dimensions of the input data tensors while operating in a remote worker (Ryffel et al., 2018).

For remote tokenization through PySyft, we modified the model to carry these inputs as static non-trainable parameters embedded in the form of tensor buffers. Using PySyft, we can move a model between the remote workers and the central worker using the API calls. Initially, these APIs were developed to handle the trainable parameters of the models among workers involved in federated learning. We contributed to the PySyft framework's codebase by developing a federated BERT tokenizer method, which handles the movement of

[5] `http://www.openmined.org/`

	Automatically annotated				Manually annotated			
	strict	exact	type	partial	strict	exact	type	partial
precision	0.64	0.72	0.70	0.74	0.55	0.56	0.68	0.79
recall	0.62	0.69	0.68	0.72	0.56	0.56	0.68	0.80
F1-score	0.64	0.70	0.69	0.73	0.55	0.56	0.68	0.80

Table 5: Test accuracy of the BERT-based NER model on both test sets

non-trainable parameters and allows full remote functionality of the model. Our implementation of the *BERT-base* model for remote operation will be released for further research.

5.2 Training Scenarios

We deploy two settings of FL to share training data in a privacy-preserved manner. In practice one of these scenarios might be preferred depending on how much trusted the central worker is.

- federated/central: A trusted central operator can receive data batches from remote data holders
- federated/remote: A mistrusted central operator sends model to a remote data holders

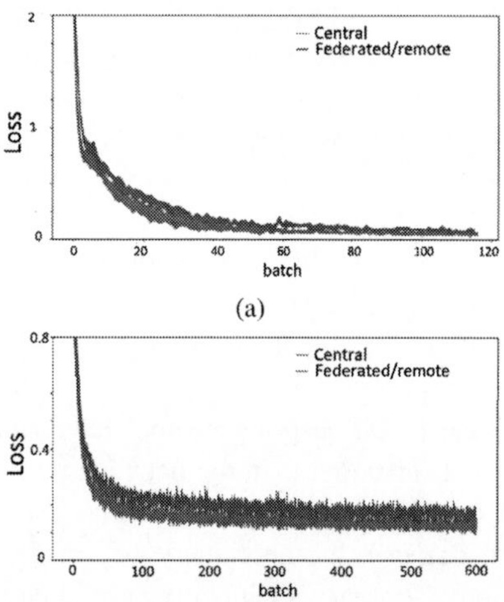

(a)

(b)

Figure 4: Training loss for central vs federated/remote on a) CoNLL-2003 and b) WikiPII dataset

In scenario 1, the operator is trusted to receive data from remote sources and updates the model in the central location. Data batches from distributed sources are called using the federated training iterator. Received data batches contribute to forward pass and back-propagation operations. Then the operator discards the data batch as agreed. Here the operator has full control over the data batches, and the BERT tokenizer works in its typical mode. The only different operations with respect to central training are data transfers from the remote workers towards the central worker. These transfers might lead to information loss because of data compression. Also, from machine learning perspective, distributed data cannot be shuffled randomly and data batches might be imbalanced which has an impact on the final performance of the model.

In scenario 2, the operator is not fully trusted, so the batch of data can not be fully transferred to the central operator. Federated training iterator holds the locations of the data holders or remote workers. The model owned by the central operator is sent to the remote worker and allowed to be remotely executed. Only the central operator's commands are allowed to reach the remote worker guaranteeing the central operator is not breaching into the data. In this scenario, we use our remote tokenization method. Interactions for this training involve sending the model, sending commands to execute the model, and receiving the trained model parameters back. Model weights are received back by the central operator after training for all the batches of data belonging to the remote worker. Then the model is sent to the other workers. An epoch is completed when the model cycles all the workers.

5.3 Performance of Model Trained with Distributed Data and Noisy Labels

To gain insight into the impact of distributed training on NER models' performance, besides the WikiPII dataset, we trained our model on the widely used NER dataset, CoNLL-2003. Similar to our central training (Section 4.2), we restrict our experiments to one epoch of training. We simulated both scenarios with only two virtual workers and recorded the training loss to investigate how remote learning impacts the model's convergence. Also, for simplicity, we assume the remote workers' availability at all the times a central worker requests their computational resources for training, which might not be the real-world scenario and will require planning and robustness.

We observed that the case of federated/central

Dataset/Setting	no. of workers	F1 score
CoNLL2003		
central	N/A	0.90 ±0.005
federated/remote	2	0.85 ±0.003
federated/central	2	0.90 ±0.008
WikiPII		
central	N/A	0.70 ±0.006
federated/remote	2	0.56 ±0.02
federated/central	2	0.70 ±0.01

Table 6: Exact F1-score for central vs federated model

training does not impact the convergence of the model. Figures 4a and 4b show the convergence of the loss when model trained on two workers in federated/remote scenario compared to the typical centralized training, for both CoNLL2003 and WikiPII. In the case of CoNLL2003, where the annotations are of gold-standard quality, the federated training does not significantly impact the model's convergence. In WikiPII, with noisy labels, federated/remote training leads to higher loss function values. However, this impact is not detrimental.

The exact F-scores trained under our FL implementations are summarized in Table 6. We observed very close final model performance between the federated learning with centrally operated and typical centralized training. Federated training with the mistrusted central operator deviates from central training, with higher loss convergence values and a reduced final performance score, for both CoNLL2003 and WikiPII datasets. This observation can be explained by the loss of information in weight compression while transferring the model.

5.4 Effect of Dataset Size

Federated learning is most useful where multiple data holders participate in the training process. In reality, different distributed sources contributing to training can carry imbalanced amounts of data and features, which can have a negative impact on the results. Here we measure the effect of increasing the dataset size by increasing the number of workers. We randomly divided the training dataset among ten workers and, starting from 2 workers, increased the number of workers participating in the training process. Figure 5 shows the change of different types of F-score as more workers are utilized, and the dataset size increases as a result. We used the federated/central scenario here, which was shown to achieve comparable performance to central training. To control for the random sampling, we repeat each experiment 10 times and average the acquired F1-score. The error plot in Figure 5 demonstrates this experiment's final results for all the metrics.

In general, we observed that when the size of the noisy annotated data increases, higher performances are achieved. Since automatic labelling of data is inexpensive, generating and sharing noisy labelled data is a promising way of achieving high-quality models. However, note that the standard deviation of F-scores can be considerable. This observation indicates that the imbalances of distributed data can drastically impact the final model.

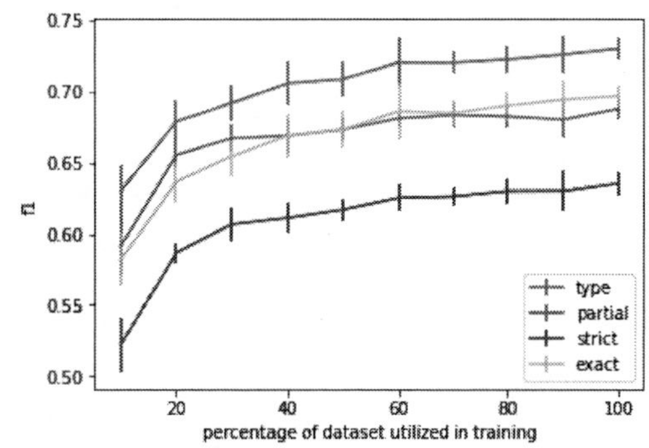

Figure 5: F1-scores vs. the training dataset size as more workers participate in federated/central training

6 Discussion

In this work, our goal is to use the historical data accumulated in an organization to build a customized NER for a human-in-the-loop PII recognition tool. We expect that this tool can significantly decrease the cost of manual extraction by locating PII entities in the free text.

First, we assume that the organization has access to a corpus of unstructured documents along with the structured dataset containing their corresponding PII entities. We propose that these parallel datasets can be used to create a noisy annotated training set. Our method of automatic annotation is based on matching of phrases and the raw data is not exposed to a third party for annotation. Using Wikipedia biography pages as an example, we show the feasibility of creating a noisy annotated dataset and training a PII recognition model in a privacy-preserved fashion. Our automatic annotation is inexpensive. Therefore it can generate large volumes of annotated datasets to compensate for the label noise. This is in line with previous work showing that deep learning is robust against noise when trained with massive noisy datasets (Rolnick et al., 2017).

Furthermore, we looked at the feasibility of distributed training in cases that multiple organizations have similar datasets and are willing to collaborate to build more robust models but cannot share the data due to privacy concerns. We showed that where the operator is trusted, distributed training will not affect performance regardless of the annotation quality. For both CoNLL2003 (clean annotations) and our WikiPII dataset (noisy annotations), the F-score of NER models does not suffer from distributed training. However, when the operator is not trusted, the F-score is impacted and the drop of F-score is more significant in the case of the noisy dataset. In model transfer, all the parameter tensors of the model go through the simplification, serialization and compression steps followed by decompression, de-serialization and decompression steps. We suspect this mechanism affects the precision of the weights. In future work, a rigorous analysis should be carried out to analyze the effect of object transfers in a distributed system.

Lastly, in the federated/central scenario, we showed that the increase in the dataset size is a promising way to achieve higher accuracies. Distributed training allows organizations to share their data which results in a bigger size of the data. We conclude that there is a trade-off between the drop in performance because of the distributed training and the increase in performance because of the higher volume of data.

This work has limitations. NER is a very challenging task, and it is difficult to achieve a fully reliable NER model for a sensitive task such as PII extraction. Also, even highly accurate NER models can be vulnerable to adversarial attacks (Zhang et al., 2020). For this reason, throughout this work, we only envisioned this system to assist human annotators by locating the entities and suggest a highly likely tag. Although this system does not reach very high performance, it is still instrumental in reducing the cost of PII extraction when compared to a fully manual procedure. We only considered a BERT-based NER model, but the general idea applies to other transformer-based NER models. In future, an ensemble of different techniques should be considered to improve the utility of the system.

7 Conclusion

We propose an inexpensive and privacy-preserved method that automatically annotates parallel structured/unstructured datasets to train a customized NER models. The final models can be used to decrease the cost of manual extraction of PII elements by preprocessing the documents in a human-in-the-loop setting. Our results demonstrate that federated training is a promising tool to compensate for label noise by increasing the volume of the noisy labeled dataset.

Acknowledgement

We would like to thank IMRSV Data Labs for partial funding and support in manual annotation. We also acknowledge Mitacs for partially funding this project.

References

Tuomas Aura, Thomas A Kuhn, and Michael Roe. 2006. Scanning electronic documents for personally identifiable information. In *Proceedings of the 5th ACM workshop on Privacy in electronic society*, pages 41–50.

Yukun Chen, Thomas A Lasko, Qiaozhu Mei, Joshua C Denny, and Hua Xu. 2015. A study of active learning methods for named entity recognition in clinical text. *Journal of biomedical informatics*, 58:11–18.

Nancy Chinchor and Beth Sundheim. 1993. MUC-5 evaluation metrics. In *Fifth Message Understanding Conference (MUC-5): Proceedings of a Conference Held in Baltimore, Maryland, August 25-27, 1993.*

Jason PC Chiu and Eric Nichols. 2016. Named entity recognition with bidirectional lstm-cnns. In *Transactions of the Association for Computational Linguistics*, volume 4, pages 357–370. MIT Press.

Zhenjin Dai, Xutao Wang, Pin Ni, Yuming Li, Gangmin Li, and Xuming Bai. 2019. Named entity recognition using BERT-BiLSTM-CRF for chinese electronic health records. In *2019 12th international congress on image and signal processing, biomedical engineering and informatics (cisp-bmei)*, pages 1–5. IEEE.

Jacob Devlin, Ming-Wei Chang, Kenton Lee, and Kristina Toutanova. 2018. Bert: Pre-training of deep bidirectional transformers for language understanding. *arXiv preprint arXiv:1810.04805*.

Kathleen C Fraser, Isar Nejadgholi, Berry De Bruijn, Muqun Li, Astha LaPlante, and Khaldoun Zine El Abidine. 2019. Extracting umls concepts from medical text using general and domain-specific deep learning models. *arXiv preprint arXiv:1910.01274*.

Jinlan Fu, Pengfei Liu, and Qi Zhang. 2020. Rethinking generalization of neural models: A named entity recognition case study. In *Proceedings of the AAAI Conference on Artificial Intelligence*, volume 34, pages 7732–7739.

Filip Graliński, Krzysztof Jassem, Michał Marcińczuk, and Paweł Wawrzyniak. 2009. Named entity recognition in machine anonymization. *Recent Advances in Intelligent Information Systems*, pages 247–260.

Fadi Hassan, Josep Domingo-Ferrer, and Jordi Soria-Comas. 2018. Anonymization of unstructured data via named-entity recognition. In *International conference on modeling decisions for artificial intelligence*, pages 296–305. Springer.

Clete A Kushida, Deborah A Nichols, Rik Jadrnicek, Ric Miller, James K Walsh, and Kara Griffin. 2012. Strategies for de-identification and anonymization of electronic health record data for use in multicenter research studies. *Medical care*, 50(Suppl):S82.

Tian Li, Anit Kumar Sahu, Ameet Talwalkar, and Virginia Smith. 2020. Federated learning: Challenges, methods, and future directions. *IEEE Signal Processing Magazine*, 37(3):50–60.

Xiao-Bai Li and Jialun Qin. 2017. Anonymizing and sharing medical text records. *Information Systems Research*, 28(2):332–352.

Gang Luo, Xiaojing Huang, Chin-Yew Lin, and Zaiqing Nie. 2015. Joint named entity recognition and disambiguation. In *Proceedings of the 2015 Conference on Empirical Methods in Natural Language Processing*, page 879–888, USA. Association for Computational Linguistics.

Ahmadreza Mosallanezhad, Ghazaleh Beigi, and Huan Liu. 2019. Deep reinforcement learning-based text anonymization against private-attribute inference. In *Proceedings of the 2019 Conference on Empirical Methods in Natural Language Processing and the 9th International Joint Conference on Natural Language Processing (EMNLP-IJCNLP)*, pages 2360–2369. Association for Computational Linguistics.

Isar Nejadgholi, Kathleen C. Fraser, and Berry De Bruijn. 2020. Extensive error analysis and a learning-based evaluation of medical entity recognition systems to approximate user experience. In *The 19th SIGBioMed Workshop on Biomedical Language Processing (BioNLP2020)*, volume 19, pages 177–186.

Joel Nothman, Nicky Ringland, Will Radford, Tara Murphy, and James R Curran. 2013. Learning multilingual named entity recognition from wikipedia. In *Artificial Intelligence*, volume 194, pages 151–175. Elsevier.

Arttu Oksanen, J Tuominen, E Mäkelä, M Tamper, Aki Hietanen, and Eero Hyvönen. 2019. Semantic finlex: Transforming, publishing, and using finnish legislation and case law as linked open data on the web. *Knowledge of the Law in the Big Data Age*, 317:212–228.

Alexandre Passos, Vineet Kumar, and Andrew McCallum. 2014. Lexicon infused phrase embeddings for named entity resolution. In *Proceedings of the Eighteenth Conference on Computational Natural Language Learning*, pages 78–86.

Alexander Ratner, Stephen H Bach, Henry Ehrenberg, Jason Fries, Sen Wu, and Christopher Ré. 2017. Snorkel: Rapid training data creation with weak supervision. In *Proceedings of the VLDB Endowment. International Conference on Very Large Data Bases*, volume 11, page 269. NIH Public Access.

Lev Retinov and Dan Roth. 2009. Design challenges and misconceptions in named entity recognition. In *Proceedings of the Thirteenth Conference on Computational Natural Language Learning (CoNLL)*, page 147–155, USA. Association for Computational Linguistics.

David Rolnick, Andreas Veit, Serge Belongie, and Nir Shavit. 2017. Deep learning is robust to massive label noise. *arXiv preprint arXiv:1705.10694*.

Theo Ryffel, Andrew Trask, Morten Dahl, Bobby Wagner, Jason Mancuso, Daniel Rueckert, and Jonathan Passerat-Palmbach. 2018. A generic framework for privacy preserving deep learning. *arXiv preprint arXiv:1811.04017*.

Erik F Sang and Fien De Meulder. 2003. Introduction to the conll-2003 shared task: Language-independent named entity recognition. In *Proceedings of the 7th Conference on Natural Language Learning, Edmonton, Canada*, pages 142—147.

Isabel Segura Bedmar, Paloma Martínez, and María Herrero Zazo. 2013. Semeval-2013 task 9: Extraction of drug-drug interactions from biomedical texts (ddiextraction 2013). Association for Computational Linguistics.

Satoshi Sekine and Hitoshi Isahara. 1999. IREX project overview. In *Proceedings of the IREX Workshop*, pages 7–12. Citeseer.

Richard Tzong-Han Tsai, Shih-Hung Wu, Wen-Chi Chou, Yu-Chun Lin, Ding He, Jieh Hsiang, Ting-Yi Sung, and Wen-Lian Hsu. 2006. Various criteria in the evaluation of biomedical named entity recognition. In *BMC bioinformatics*, volume 7, page 92. Springer.

Qiang Yang, Yang Liu, Tianjian Chen, and Yongxin Tong. 2019. Federated machine learning: Concept and applications. *ACM Transactions on Intelligent Systems and Technology (TIST)*, 10(2):1–19.

Wei Emma Zhang, Quan Z Sheng, Ahoud Alhazmi, and Chenliang Li. 2020. Adversarial attacks on deep-learning models in natural language processing: A survey. *ACM Transactions on Intelligent Systems and Technology (TIST)*, 11(3):1–41.

Using Confidential Data for Domain Adaptation of Neural Machine Translation

Sohyung Kim **Arianna Bisazza** **Fatih Turkmen**
University of Groningen
s.kim22@student.rug.nl
{a.bisazza, f.turkmen}@rug.nl

Abstract

We study the problem of domain adaptation in Neural Machine Translation (NMT) when domain-specific data cannot be shared due to confidentiality or copyright issues. As a first step, we propose to fragment data into phrase pairs and use a random sample to fine-tune a generic NMT model instead of the full sentences. Despite the loss of long segments for the sake of confidentiality protection, we find that NMT quality can considerably benefit from this adaptation, and that further gains can be obtained with a simple tagging technique.

1 Introduction

The availability of in-domain data remains essential to ensure the quality of Neural Machine Translation (NMT), especially in technical domains (Koehn and Knowles, 2017). However, obtaining such data is often challenging, and in many real-world scenarios this is further aggravated by data confidentiality or copyright concerns. In fact, when data content is sensitive, the owner may simply deny providing its Translation Memories to the translation company it is hiring (Cancedda, 2012). This can lead to considerably worse MT quality, higher post-editing efforts, and subsequently higher translation costs for the data owners themselves.

When the complete data cannot be shared in its original form, releasing *fragmented* data can be considered as a compromise. The most well-known example of releasing fragmented data is *Google N-gram* (Michel et al., 2011). N-gram tables consisting of sequences of n words and their counts in a given corpus were routinely used to train count-based language models (Kneser and Ney, 1995; Brants et al., 2007) before the advent of neural methods. However, N-grams are not optimal for training state-of-the-art NLP models such as sequence-to-sequence LSTM (Bahdanau et al., 2015) or Transformers (Vaswani et al., 2017). In fact, one of the main strengths of these models is the ability of handling arbitrarily long contexts, which would be hindered by the use of fragmented data. In this paper, we take a pragmatic approach and ask: If the data owner can *only* release fragmented data due to confidentiality issues, can this still benefit downstream NMT quality in any way?

Motivated by the brittleness of NMT in out-of-domain settings (Koehn and Knowles, 2017) and the increasing availability of large pre-trained models (Ng et al., 2019), we focus on the task of adapting a strong-performing general-domain NMT system to various technical domains. We show that fine-tuning on *phrase pairs* can be a viable solution to exploit confidential data, but the scale of improvements varies strongly across target domains.

2 Background

To our knowledge, the use of confidential data in MT has not received much attention recently. Cancedda (2012) proposed an encryption-based (one-time pad) method for phrase-based statistical machine translation (PB-SMT). However, PB-SMT is nowadays clearly outperformed by NMT (Bentivogli et al., 2016), which function completely differently and therefore require new solutions to preserve data confidentiality.

In the broader context of NLP, secure multi-party computation (Feng et al., 2020) and homomorphic encryption (Al Badawi et al., 2020) have been used to provide strong privacy guarantees. Since these cryptographic methods incur high performance penalties (see (Riazi et al., 2019) for an overview of their performance in deep learning), more recent proposals have focused on the careful use of simpler cryptographic primitives while training a model over encrypted text due to confidentiality reasons. For instance, TextHide (Huang et al., 2020) allows to perform natural language understanding tasks while requiring the participants to complete an encryption step in a federated setting. The aforementioned studies mostly focus on

Proceedings of the 58th Annual Meeting of the Association for Computational Linguistics, pages 46–52
July 5–10, 2020. ©2020 Association for Computational Linguistics
https://doi.org/10.26615/978-954-452-056-4_006

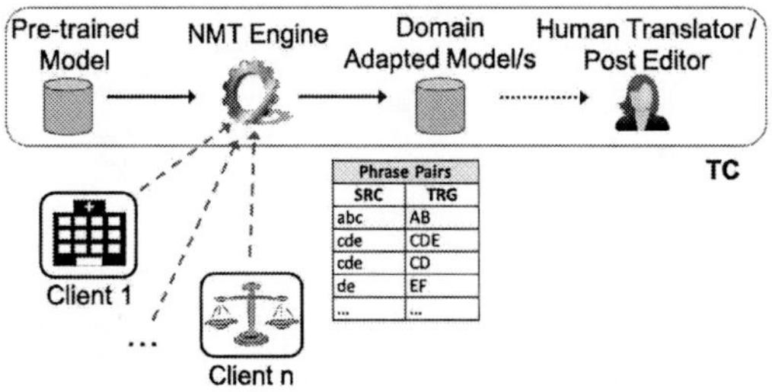

Figure 1: Motivating scenario: a Translation Company (TC) uses confidential data from its clients to adapt a pre-trained generic NMT system to different technical (e.g. medical, legal) domains.

preventing explicit/implicit leakage of partial information while training the models. By contrast, we explore the possibility of using fragmented data to improve state-of-the-art NMT applications.

Scenario As illustrated in Figure 1, we consider a common case where a translation company (TC) provides professional services based on a pipeline of NMT and human post-editing. TC wants to improve the quality of its NMT models by training or adapting them on the clients' previously translated data. Due to confidentiality concerns, the clients only provide their data in a fragmented form as a compromise. If this kind of data can be used to improve the NMT model, both the clients and the company will benefit by abating human post-editing costs. Thus, we want to study the possibility of sharing fragmented data for improving utility while preserving the confidentiality of data.

Threat Model We assume an honest but curious model in which the receiver of the partial data (e.g. the translation company) is untrusted or only partially trusted. The main threat we focus on is the **full reconstruction** of the original text from a list of given n-grams of phrases rather than the protection of partial information (e.g. key phrases (Hard et al., 2018), names, social security numbers). This setting is useful in various contexts where only partial data release is desired such as copyright protection. Examples of text where sensitive information is encoded in long sequences (sentences or paragraphs) include patent applications, as well as not (yet) publicly available product analysis reports or drug reaction reports.

3 Approach

Releasing fragmented data in the form of N-grams has a long tradition in NLP (Michel et al., 2011). However, fixed-size N-gram extraction is not directly applicable to parallel data because it breaks translation equivalence with the target side. As a solution, we propose to use *phrase pairs* (Koehn et al., 2003) as a text fragmentation method.

3.1 Phrase Pairs

Like N-grams, phrases are short sequences of consecutive words extracted from the input sentences. Unlike N-grams, phrases are always extracted in pairs from source-target sentence pairs in a way that is *consistent* with their word-level alignment. Formally, a phrase pair $(\bar{f}, \bar{e})$ is consistent with word alignment A if all source words $f_1, \cdots, f_n$ in $\bar{f}$ that have alignment points in A are connected with target words $e_1, \cdots, e_m$ in $\bar{e}$ and viceversa (Koehn et al., 2003; Koehn, 2009). As Figure 2 illustrates, the words of the target language (German) are first automatically aligned (grey connecting lines) with the words of the source language (English) by a statistical alignment model. Then, phrase pairs of various lengths (denoted by boxes) are extracted.

Phrase pairs and their statistics constitute the main component of PB-SMT systems, together with the target language model. In this work, however, we only use phrase extraction as a text fragmentation technique. After extraction, we shuffle the large set of phrase pairs extracted from the whole dataset and, finally, discard a random sample of phrase pairs (e.g. 50%) to preserve confidentiality. In the example of Figure 2, this would mean protecting the hypothetically sensitive connection between the drug name (*Abraxane*) and its reported side effect (*tiredness*).

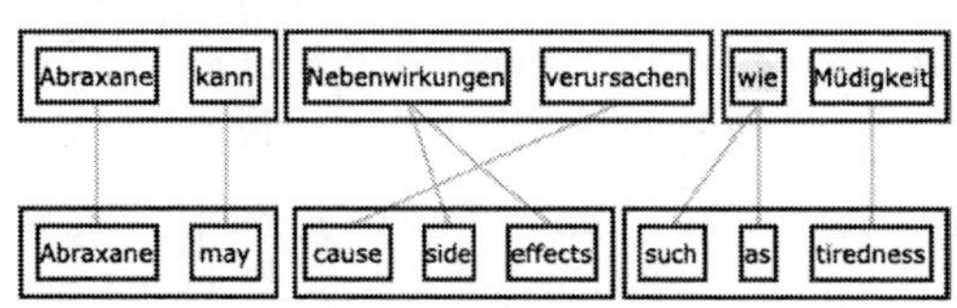

Figure 2: Example sentence pair from the EMEA corpus with extracted phrase pairs of maximum length 3 (every black box is a phrase). Grey lines denote word alignment. Shorter phrases imply more data protection.

3.2 Domain Adaptation

NMT models are trained on full sentences, and their ability to capture large context is one of their main strengths compared to classical SMT approaches. As a result, training NMT on fragmented data is likely to lead to a very poor performance. Nonetheless, we postulate that phrase pairs may still contain very valuable information for the *adaptation* of a general-domain system to a specific target domain. In fact, much of domain adaptation has to do with learning new words or short phrases, as well as new senses for known words and phrases (Irvine et al., 2013). As the domain adaptation technique, we choose fine-tuning (Luong et al., 2015; Sennrich et al., 2016b) which consists of continuing training a previously trained model on a, typically smaller, in-domain dataset.

We start by directly fine-tuning a general-domain NMT system on a random sample of phrase pairs (occurrences, not types) extracted from the in-domain dataset. Since this is expected to bias the model to produce shorter sentences, we also experiment with a simple phrase tagging technique (Sennrich et al., 2016a) so that the model may learn to represent the special nature of phrases and be less inclined to produce short outputs when translating full sentences in the test phase.

4 Experimental setup

We evaluate our approach on German-English in the domains of medicine descriptions, software manuals, and EU legislation. To simulate a realistic production setup, we start from a strong NMT system pre-trained on large amounts (28M sentences) of publicly available data.

Baseline NMT We use the Transformer-based system (Vaswani et al., 2017) pre-trained by Facebook for the WMT'19 news translation task (Ng et al., 2019)[1] and released as part of the Fairseq toolkit (Ott et al., 2019). This model was ranked first in the WMT'19 news competition (Barrault et al., 2019) with a BLEU score of 40.8.

Datasets We simulate confidential translation data by using publicly available datasets from three technical domains:[2] EMEA (medical), GNOME (software) and JRC-Acquis (legal) (Tiedemann, 2012; Steinberger et al., 2006).[3] Data statistics are shown in Table 1. Following the Fairseq model pipeline, we segment our data with FastBPE byte-pair encoding (Sennrich et al., 2016c).[4]

Type	Domain	#sent	#tok(DE)	#tok(EN)
Train	EMEA	10k	199k	209k
	GNOME		179k	194k
	JRC		279k	396k
Valid	EMEA	150	3k	3k
	GNOME		3k	3k
	JRC		4k	5k
Test	EMEA	2k	38k	42k
	GNOME		29k	30k
	JRC		53k	82k

Table 1: Size of datasets used in our fine-tuning experiments. The baseline NMT model was pre-trained on a separate corpus of 28M sentence pairs, not shown here.

Phrase extraction We first word-align the in-domain datasets using FASTALIGN (Dyer et al., 2013)[5] and compute the union of source-to-target and target-to-source word alignment links (known as union symmetrization heuristic) to obtain the alignment A. Then we use the phrase extraction utility from the MOSES phrase-based SMT toolkit (Koehn et al., 2007)[6] to extract all phrases consistent with A. After the phrase extraction step, our dataset has been fragmented into a list of aligned phrases of various lengths. We experiment with a maximum source-side phrase length of either 4 or 7 words, and in both cases we randomly discard 50% of the extracted phrases (occurrences, not types).

Fine-Tuning During fine-tuning, we provide phrase pairs to the models as if they were sentence pairs. Note that this data is shuffled and has many duplicates. Additionally, we experiment with a simple tagging technique by adding <P> and </P> at the front and end of each phrase respectively, in both source and target side. During testing, full sentences with no tags are given to the model.

We apply the hyper-parameters described by Ng et al. (2019) with only a few adjustments inspired from previous work on fine-tuning regularization (Miceli Barone et al., 2017) and tuned on a small (full-sentence) validation set in each domain (150 sentences, see Table 1). Specifically, learning rate is divided by 4 (0.000175), weight decay rate is set to 0.0001 and dropout probability to 0.2. The same small validation set is used for early stopping.

[1] https://github.com/pytorch/fairseq/tree/master/examples/translation

[2] To simulate a professional translation scenario, we split the datasets by documents. We release the benchmarks at https://github.com/Sohyo/Using-Confidential-Data-for-NMT

[3] https://opus.nlpl.eu

[4] https://github.com/glample/fastBPE

[5] https://github.com/clab/fast_align

[6] http://www.statmt.org/moses

		Fine-Tuning				
	Baseline	**Max length 4**		**Max length 7**		***Original data***
	(No fine-tuning)	**No tag**	**Tag**	**No tag**	**Tag**	*(Full sentences)*
EMEA	35.5	39.1	40.5	41.5	37.2	*45.2*
GNOME	29.8	36.0	37.0	35.8	36.8	*38.9*
JRC	29.0	29.4	30.0	29.2	29.7	*54.7*

Table 2: BLEU scores of German-English NMT in three different domains: medical (EMEA), software (GNOME), and legal (JRC). The baseline is the pre-trained Fairseq WMT19 news system (Ng et al., 2019) based on Transformer (Vaswani et al., 2017) and ranked first in the WMT19 competition.

5 Results

We evaluate the quality of NMT models by BLEU (Papineni et al., 2002) computed with SACRE-BLEU (Post, 2018). The phrase-adapted models are compared to the non-adapted baseline (Ng et al., 2019), and to fine-tuning on the original (non fragmented) dataset in order to determine the maximum possible gains. Results are reported in Table 2.

Our main finding is that phrase pairs can indeed be used to fine-tune a NMT model without any changes to the architecture or the need of specific fine-tuning algorithms. The BLEU gains over the non-adapted baseline vary between +7.0 on EMEA and +1.0 on JRC. This is relevant for our scenario because even translation companies without significant in-house NMT expertise could easily apply our solution to their workflow. Our approach is also applicable in cases where TC uses NMT as an outsourced (cloud-based) service, by sending the provider phrase pairs instead of full sentences for model adaptation.

Effect of phrase tagging The addition of tags appear to improve NMT quality in most cases. Figure 3 shows that tagging yields slightly longer system outputs, suggesting the model indeed learned to associate the <P> tag with shorter training samples. While differences look small, they have a large impact on BLEU because of the Brevity Penalty (Papineni et al., 2002). As a notable exception to this positive trend, BLEU score decreases with tagging on EMEA (max length 7). We are currently investigating this result further.

Effect of phrase length We expected longer phrases to be considerably more useful for fine-tuning, at the expense of less confidentiality protection. By contrast, increasing the maximum length from 4 to 7 does not have a positive effect on BLEU but actually lowers it in the GNOME and JRC domains. This counter-intuitive result may be due to the fact that increasing the maximum length leads to a much larger number of extracted phrases that are redundant and overlapping. Previous work on lexicon-augmented NMT also reported negative results when fine-tuning on very large numbers of segments (Thompson et al., 2019b). In future work, we plan to experiment with minimum phrase length as a way to reduce the total number of phrase pairs.

Domain differences The benefits of fine-tuning on phrases appear to vary strongly across domains: on EMEA we obtain large gains but there is still space for improvement, on GNOME our approach nears the ceiling of fine-tuning on the original data, whereas on JRC gains are small and scores remain very far from the ceiling. To explain these results, we inspected our datasets and specifically looked for peculiarities of the JRC dataset. We find that JRC is rather different in terms of sentence length distribution, with much longer sentences on average. As shown in Figure 3, only fine-tuning on the original data leads to reasonably long outputs, whereas baseline and phrase-adapted systems all generate sentences that are, on average, about 10 words shorter than they should be. This suggests that our tagging technique is not sufficient to address the shorter-output bias in a robust way. Recent techniques to prevent overfitting during fine-tuning (Kirkpatrick et al., 2017; Thompson et al., 2019a) may overcome this problem in future work.

6 Conclusions

We have studied the problem of domain adaptation of NMT models when domain-specific data cannot be shared due to confidentiality or copyright concerns. Inspired by a common NLP practice of sharing confidential data in the form of N-grams (Michel et al., 2011), we propose to use phrase extraction (Koehn et al., 2003), shuffling and subsampling as a data fragmentation technique for translation data. Our experiments on three different

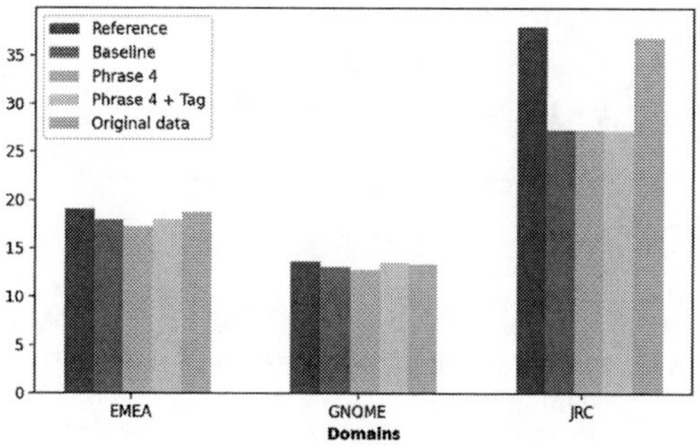

Figure 3: Average length (in tokens) of reference translations and outputs of different NMT systems, including a non-fine-tuned baseline and four differently fine-tuned systems.

domains show that this type of data can be used to fine-tune NMT models leading to considerable improvements on top of a strong baseline and further gains when a simple phrase tagging technique is used. We also find that the magnitude of these gains varies largely across domains, which we tentatively attribute to the different length profiles of our datasets (e.g. legal domain has much longer sentences than the other domains).

While our results show that text fragmentation is indeed compatible with modern machine translation systems adaptation, more work needs to be done before our method can be applied on actual sensitive data. To this end, we plan to determine metrics for the quantification of confidentiality protection (or violation) when an adversary tries to reconstruct the original documents. Our starting point for this direction would be Gallé and Tealdi (2015), who presented a technique for this purpose only in the context of (monolingual) N-grams.

Acknowledgements

We are grateful to Global Textware for giving us early input on the motivating scenario of this work. Arianna Bisazza was partly funded by the Netherlands Organization for Scientific Research (NWO) under project number 639.021.646.

References

Ahmad Al Badawi, Louie Hoang, Chan Fook Mun, Kim Laine, and Khin Mi Mi Aung. 2020. Privft: Private and fast text classification with homomorphic encryption. *IEEE Access*, 8:226544–226556.

Dzmitry Bahdanau, Kyunghyun Cho, and Yoshua Bengio. 2015. Neural machine translation by jointly learning to align and translate. *CoRR*, abs/1409.0473.

Loïc Barrault, Ondřej Bojar, Marta R. Costa-jussà, Christian Federmann, Mark Fishel, Yvette Graham, Barry Haddow, Matthias Huck, Philipp Koehn, Shervin Malmasi, Christof Monz, Mathias Müller, Santanu Pal, Matt Post, and Marcos Zampieri. 2019. Findings of the 2019 conference on machine translation (WMT19). In *Proceedings of the Fourth Conference on Machine Translation (Volume 2: Shared Task Papers, Day 1)*, pages 1–61, Florence, Italy. Association for Computational Linguistics.

Luisa Bentivogli, Arianna Bisazza, Mauro Cettolo, and Marcello Federico. 2016. Neural versus phrase-based machine translation quality: a case study. In *Proceedings of the 2016 Conference on Empirical Methods in Natural Language Processing*, pages 257–267, Austin, Texas. Association for Computational Linguistics.

Thorsten Brants, Ashok C. Popat, Peng Xu, Franz J. Och, and Jeffrey Dean. 2007. Large language models in machine translation. In *Proceedings of the 2007 Joint Conference on Empirical Methods in Natural Language Processing and Computational Natural Language Learning (EMNLP-CoNLL)*, pages 858–867, Prague, Czech Republic. Association for Computational Linguistics.

Nicola Cancedda. 2012. Private access to phrase tables for statistical machine translation. In *Proceedings of the 50th Annual Meeting of the Association for Computational Linguistics (Volume 2: Short Papers)*, pages 23–27, Jeju Island, Korea. Association for Computational Linguistics.

Chris Dyer, Victor Chahuneau, and Noah A. Smith. 2013. A simple, fast, and effective reparameterization of IBM model 2. In *Proceedings of the 2013 Conference of the North American Chapter of the Association for Computational Linguistics: Human Language Technologies*, pages 644–648, Atlanta, Georgia. Association for Computational Linguistics.

Qi Feng, Debiao He, Zhe Liu, Huaqun Wang, and Kim-Kwang Raymond Choo. 2020. Securenlp: A system for multi-party privacy-preserving natural language processing. *IEEE Transactions on Information Forensics and Security*, 15:3709–3721.

Matthias Gallé and Matías Tealdi. 2015. Reconstructing textual documents from n-grams. In *Proceedings of the 21th ACM SIGKDD International Conference on Knowledge Discovery and Data Mining*, pages 329–338.

Andrew Hard, Kanishka Rao, Rajiv Mathews, Swaroop Ramaswamy, Françoise Beaufays, Sean Augenstein, Hubert Eichner, Chloé Kiddon, and Daniel Ramage. 2018. Federated learning for mobile keyboard prediction. *arXiv preprint arXiv:1811.03604*.

Yangsibo Huang, Zhao Song, Danqi Chen, Kai Li, and Sanjeev Arora. 2020. Texthide: Tackling data privacy for language understanding tasks. In *Proceedings of the 2020 Conference on Empirical Methods in Natural Language Processing: Findings, EMNLP 2020, Online Event, 16-20 November 2020*, pages 1368–1382. Association for Computational Linguistics.

Ann Irvine, John Morgan, Marine Carpuat, Hal Daumé III, and Dragos Munteanu. 2013. Measuring machine translation errors in new domains. *Transactions of the Association for Computational Linguistics*, 1:429–440.

James Kirkpatrick, Razvan Pascanu, Neil Rabinowitz, Joel Veness, Guillaume Desjardins, Andrei A Rusu, Kieran Milan, John Quan, Tiago Ramalho, Agnieszka Grabska-Barwinska, et al. 2017. Overcoming catastrophic forgetting in neural networks. *Proceedings of the national academy of sciences*, 114(13):3521–3526.

R. Kneser and H. Ney. 1995. Improved backing-off for m-gram language modeling. In *1995 International Conference on Acoustics, Speech, and Signal Processing*, volume 1, pages 181–184 vol.1.

Philipp Koehn. 2009. *Statistical Machine Translation*. Cambridge University Press.

Philipp Koehn, Hieu Hoang, Alexandra Birch, Chris Callison-Burch, Marcello Federico, Nicola Bertoldi, Brooke Cowan, Wade Shen, Christine Moran, Richard Zens, Chris Dyer, Ondřej Bojar, Alexandra Constantin, and Evan Herbst. 2007. Moses: Open source toolkit for statistical machine translation. In *Proceedings of the 45th Annual Meeting of the Association for Computational Linguistics Companion Volume Proceedings of the Demo and Poster Sessions*, pages 177–180, Prague, Czech Republic. Association for Computational Linguistics.

Philipp Koehn and Rebecca Knowles. 2017. Six challenges for neural machine translation. In *Proceedings of the First Workshop on Neural Machine Translation*, pages 28–39, Vancouver. Association for Computational Linguistics.

Philipp Koehn, Franz J. Och, and Daniel Marcu. 2003. Statistical phrase-based translation. In *Proceedings of the 2003 Human Language Technology Conference of the North American Chapter of the Association for Computational Linguistics*, pages 127–133.

Minh-Thang Luong, Christopher D Manning, et al. 2015. Stanford neural machine translation systems for spoken language domains. In *Proceedings of the international workshop on spoken language translation*, pages 76–79.

Antonio Valerio Miceli Barone, Barry Haddow, Ulrich Germann, and Rico Sennrich. 2017. Regularization techniques for fine-tuning in neural machine translation. In *Proceedings of the 2017 Conference on Empirical Methods in Natural Language Processing*, pages 1489–1494, Copenhagen, Denmark. Association for Computational Linguistics.

Jean-Baptiste Michel, Yuan Kui Shen, Aviva Presser Aiden, Adrian Veres, Matthew K Gray, Joseph P Pickett, Dale Hoiberg, Dan Clancy, Peter Norvig, Jon Orwant, et al. 2011. Quantitative analysis of culture using millions of digitized books. *science*, 331(6014):176–182.

Nathan Ng, Kyra Yee, Alexei Baevski, Myle Ott, Michael Auli, and Sergey Edunov. 2019. Facebook FAIR's WMT19 news translation task submission. In *Proceedings of the Fourth Conference on Machine Translation (Volume 2: Shared Task Papers, Day 1)*, pages 314–319, Florence, Italy. Association for Computational Linguistics.

Myle Ott, Sergey Edunov, Alexei Baevski, Angela Fan, Sam Gross, Nathan Ng, David Grangier, and Michael Auli. 2019. fairseq: A fast, extensible toolkit for sequence modeling. In *Proceedings of the 2019 Conference of the North American Chapter of the Association for Computational Linguistics (Demonstrations)*, pages 48–53, Minneapolis, Minnesota. Association for Computational Linguistics.

Kishore Papineni, Salim Roukos, Todd Ward, and Wei-Jing Zhu. 2002. Bleu: a method for automatic evaluation of machine translation. In *Proceedings of the 40th Annual Meeting of the Association for Computational Linguistics*, pages 311–318, Philadelphia, Pennsylvania, USA. Association for Computational Linguistics.

Matt Post. 2018. A call for clarity in reporting BLEU scores. In *Proceedings of the Third Conference on Machine Translation: Research Papers*, pages 186–191, Brussels, Belgium. Association for Computational Linguistics.

M Sadegh Riazi, Bita Darvish Rouani, and Farinaz Koushanfar. 2019. Deep learning on private data. *IEEE Security & Privacy*, 17(6):54–63.

Rico Sennrich, Barry Haddow, and Alexandra Birch. 2016a. Controlling politeness in neural machine translation via side constraints. In *Proceedings of the 2016 Conference of the North American Chapter of the Association for Computational Linguistics: Human Language Technologies*, pages 35–40.

Rico Sennrich, Barry Haddow, and Alexandra Birch. 2016b. Improving neural machine translation models with monolingual data. In *Proceedings of the 54th Annual Meeting of the Association for Computational Linguistics (Volume 1: Long Papers)*, pages 86–96, Berlin, Germany. Association for Computational Linguistics.

Rico Sennrich, Barry Haddow, and Alexandra Birch. 2016c. Neural machine translation of rare words with subword units. In *Proceedings of the 54th Annual Meeting of the Association for Computational*

Linguistics (Volume 1: Long Papers), pages 1715–1725, Berlin, Germany. Association for Computational Linguistics.

Ralf Steinberger, Bruno Pouliquen, Anna Widiger, Camelia Ignat, Tomaz Erjavec, Dan Tufis, and Dániel Varga. 2006. The jrc-acquis: A multilingual aligned parallel corpus with 20+ languages. *arXiv preprint cs/0609058*.

Brian Thompson, Jeremy Gwinnup, Huda Khayrallah, Kevin Duh, and Philipp Koehn. 2019a. Overcoming catastrophic forgetting during domain adaptation of neural machine translation. In *Proceedings of the 2019 Conference of the North American Chapter of the Association for Computational Linguistics: Human Language Technologies, Volume 1 (Long and Short Papers)*, pages 2062–2068, Minneapolis, Minnesota. Association for Computational Linguistics.

Brian Thompson, Rebecca Knowles, Xuan Zhang, Huda Khayrallah, Kevin Duh, and Philipp Koehn. 2019b. HABLex: Human annotated bilingual lexicons for experiments in machine translation. In *Proceedings of the 2019 Conference on Empirical Methods in Natural Language Processing and the 9th International Joint Conference on Natural Language Processing (EMNLP-IJCNLP)*, pages 1382–1387, Hong Kong, China. Association for Computational Linguistics.

Jörg Tiedemann. 2012. Parallel data, tools and interfaces in opus. In *Lrec*, volume 2012, pages 2214–2218.

Ashish Vaswani, Noam Shazeer, Niki Parmar, Jakob Uszkoreit, Llion Jones, Aidan N Gomez, Łukasz Kaiser, and Illia Polosukhin. 2017. Attention is all you need. In *Advances in neural information processing systems*, pages 5998–6008.

Private Text Classification with Convolutional Neural Networks

Samuel Adams[1]**, David Melanson**[1]**, Martine De Cock**[1,2]
[1] School of Engineering and Technology
University of Washington Tacoma
{sadams,mence40,mdecock}@uw.edu
[2] Dept. of Applied Math., Computer Science and Statistics
Ghent University
martine.decock@ugent.be

Abstract

Text classifiers are regularly applied to personal texts, leaving users of these classifiers vulnerable to privacy breaches. We propose a solution for privacy-preserving text classification that is based on Convolutional Neural Networks (CNNs) and Secure Multiparty Computation (MPC). Our method enables the inference of a class label for a personal text in such a way that (1) the owner of the personal text does not have to disclose their text to anyone in an unencrypted manner, and (2) the owner of the text classifier does not have to reveal the trained model parameters to the text owner or to anyone else. To demonstrate the feasibility of our protocol for practical private text classification, we implemented it in the PyTorch-based MPC framework CrypTen, using a well-known additive secret sharing scheme in the honest-but-curious setting. We test the runtime of our privacy-preserving text classifier, which is fast enough to be used in practice.

1 Introduction

Text classification is inherently a two-party computation problem between the owner of a text classifier and the owner of a personal text. Text classifiers are used for a wide variety of purposes, such as detection of spam and misinformation, sentiment analysis, tailored advertising, surveillance, etc. In these applications, the text classifier is often owned by a company or organization who wants to keep their model private because it offers a competitive advantage and/or it was trained on a proprietary dataset. Deep learning models in particular are powerful enough to memorize specific examples from the training data (Carlini et al., 2019), hence disclosing a trained model can leak very specific information about training data. Furthermore, in applications such as spam or misinformation detection, disclosing the model would help adversaries to develop strategies for evading detection.

The common practice nowadays is therefore for the owner of the personal text to disclose their text to the company or application developer. This in turn also raises serious privacy concerns, stemming from misuse of the data by the company for purposes beyond the originally professed scope. Furthermore, while most companies make reasonable efforts to keep data private, the data itself is a valuable asset that is routinely sold when companies undergo bankruptcy and/or it can become subject of accidental or intentional public exposure (Canny, 2002; Solon, 2018; Thompson and Warzel, 2019). Data breaches and intentional misuse of data have given rise to new laws and regulations, such as the European General Data Protection Regulation (GDPR) and the California Consumer Privacy Act (CCPA), and, orthogonal to this, the use of privacy-enhancing technologies (PETs) for the development of algorithms that do not leak personal information about their inputs, thereby protecting the privacy of all the users involved.

In this paper we propose such an algorithm for private text classification that, as illustrated in Fig. 1, allows the owner of a personal text (*Bob*) to infer a label using *Alice*'s text classifier, without requiring Bob to disclose anything about his text in an unencrypted manner to Alice, and without requiring Alice to show her trained model parameters to anyone. To this end, we use Secure Multiparty Computation (MPC) (Cramer et al., 2015), an umbrella term for cryptographic approaches that allow two or more parties to jointly compute a specified output (the class label) from their private information (the classifier and the personal text) in a distributed fashion, without revealing the private information to each other.

Initial solutions for private classification of unstructured text with MPC have been proposed for logistic regression models and tree based models (Reich et al., 2019), and for Naive Bayes classifiers (Resende et al., 2021). All of this existing work relies on an MPC subprotocol for private feature extraction, in which a boolean word occurrence

Proceedings of the 58th Annual Meeting of the Association for Computational Linguistics, pages 53–58
July 5–10, 2020.
https://doi.org/10.26615/978-954-452-056-4_007

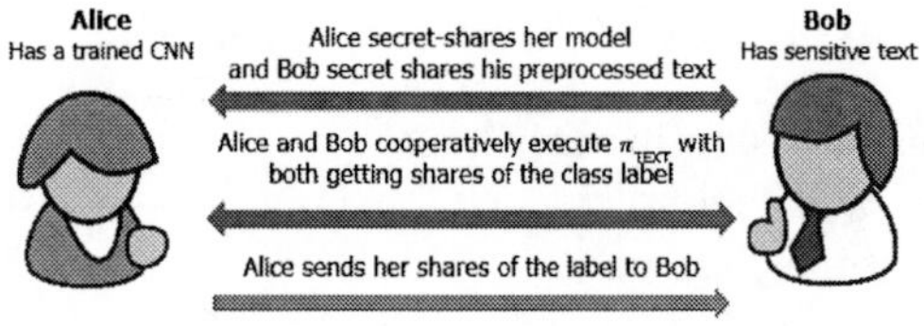

Figure 1: Private text classification process

vector is created that indicates which words from Alice's predefined vocabulary occur in Bob's text. In contrast with this, and in line with the fact that deep learning is current state-of-the-art for many tasks in natural language processing (NLP), we propose to perform MPC-based private text classification with a Convolutional Neural Network (CNN) that has been trained to extract relevant features automatically. To the best of our knowledge this has not been explored yet in the literature.

The MPC protocols for text classification with CNNs that we use in this paper, are very similar to existing MPC protocols for image classification with CNNs (Agrawal et al., 2019; Dalskov et al., 2020; Juvekar et al., 2018; Kumar et al., 2020; Mishra et al., 2020). The main distinguishing aspect is that image classification is based on 2-dimensional (2D) CNNs, while for text classification it is common to use 1-dimensional (1D) CNNs in which the filters move in only one direction. Existing MPC protocols for inference with 2D CNNs can be straightforwardly adjusted to 1D CNNs. Our main contribution is therefore in designing the first application of MPC protocols for CNN-based text classification, and in particular in addressing a question that has remained open in the literature thus far, namely to what extent such provably secure protocols can enable *accurate* and *fast* text classification.

Among deep learning architectures, our choice for CNNs is deliberate. CNNs have been successfully applied for text classification (Kim, 2014) and offer the important advantage of being computationally less intensive than Long Short-Term Memory (LSTM) networks or other state-of-the-art architectures. As such, CNNs are an excellent "MPC-friendly" starting point to explore deep learning based private text classification. In Sec. 2 we describe a multi-channel CNN architecture that we designed for sentiment analysis of product reviews. The trained CNN F is owned by Alice in Fig. 1.

In Sec. 3 we describe our MPC protocol π_{TEXT} for private text classification of Bob's text with Alice's CNN F. As the first step in this process, Bob prepares his text using preprocessing steps that are publicly known and do not depend on Alice's model F nor on the data that Alice used to train F in any way. In our prototype, the preprocessing consists of converting the text using a publicly available sentence transformer (Reimers and Gurevych, 2019). Below we refer to both Alice's CNN model parameters and Bob's preprocessed text simply as "data". At the start of π_{TEXT}, Alice and Bob send each other encrypted shares of their data. Subsequently both parties engage in MPC computations and exchange intermediate encrypted results, without learning anything about the values of the data. At the end of π_{TEXT}, Alice and Bob each have "shares" of the inferred class label. The true class label is revealed only when these shares are combined, e.g. when Alice sends her shares to Bob.

In Sec. 4 we present results obtained with an implementation of π_{TEXT} in CrypTen (Knott et al., 2020), a recently proposed MPC framework built upon PyTorch. CrypTen realizes MPC through a well-known additive secret sharing scheme (see Sec. 3) that guards against honest-but-curious adversaries. A party corrupted by such an adversary still follows the instructions of the MPC protocol but attempts to learn information about the data from the intermediate values and communications between the parties. A correctly designed MPC protocol (as π_{TEXT}) prevents such attacks from being successful. To implement π_{TEXT}, we adapted and extended existing functionality for private image classification in CrypTen to text classification with 1-dimensional (1D) convolutional layers and 1D max pooling. Our results in Tab. 2 demonstrate the practicality of π_{TEXT} as the runtimes are low enough to be used in practice.

Quantity of reviews by star rating				
1	2	3	4	5
23,783	6,890	8,308	46,693	46,410
negative			positive	

Table 1: Distribution of reviews by star rating

2 Text Classifier

Dataset. We trained Alice's model on the Software portion of the Amazon Customer Reviews Dataset.[1]

[1] https://s3.amazonaws.com/amazon-reviews-pds/readme.html

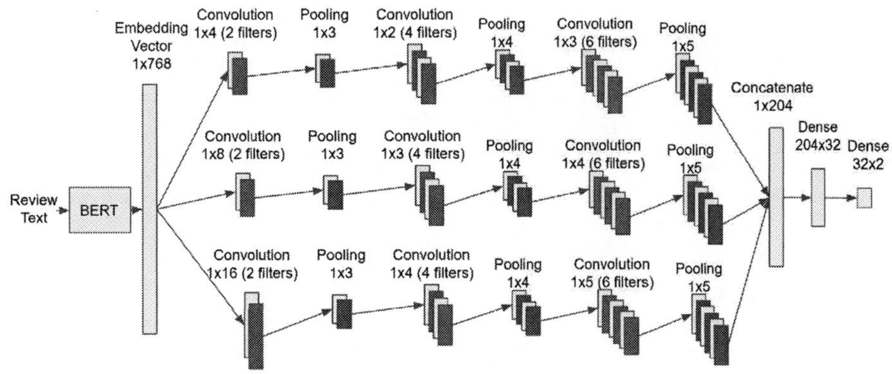

Figure 2: The structure of Alice's CNN

The data consists of product reviews for software offered on Amazon's storefront. There are 132,084 reviews total, each with an associated star rating ranging from one to five (see Tab. 1). The average length of a review is 63.6 words. We split the data into 80% for training and 20% for validation, using a stratified split to ensure the distribution of the star ratings is identical in both sets. As described below, we trained a binary classifier for sentiment analysis over this dataset, treating reviews with star ratings ≥ 4 as positive instances, and the rest as negative. We note that, with reproducibility of results in mind, we used a publicly available dataset. During deployment of our private text classification solution, it can be replaced by proprietary text data.

Model Architecture. The text classifier consists of two parts: a public sentence transformer and the private CNN belonging to Alice. The sentence transformer we employ is `stsb-distilbert-base` (Reimers and Gurevych, 2019), a model fine-tuned to produce sentence vectors. This takes as input the raw text and outputs a 768 dimensional embedding vector. As this transformer is public, Bob can also use the sentence transformer to prepare his data for classification by Alice's model. Alice's model consists of three parallel series of convolution and pooling layers, followed by fully-connected layers, ending in a sigmoid activated classification layer (see Fig. 2). This model is then trained with a learning rate of 0.002 with a batch size of 50, and loss is calculated using cross entropy. A dropout of 0.25 is added to the concatenation layer. The trained model obtains 85% accuracy on the validation data.

3 Private Text Classification

Additive Secret Sharing MPC Scheme. Protocols for Secure Multiparty Computation (MPC) enable a set of parties to jointly compute the output of a function over the private inputs of each party, without requiring any of the parties to disclose their own private inputs (Evans et al., 2018). MPC is concerned with the protocol execution coming under attack by an adversary which may corrupt one or more of the parties. In this paper we assume a set-up with two parties (Alice and Bob), one of which may be corrupted by an honest-but-curious adversary. "Honest-but-curious" means that a corrupted party still follows the instructions of the protocol, but the adversary attempts to learn private information from the internal state of the corrupted party and the messages that it receives. MPC protocols that are secure against honest-but-curious adversaries prevent such leakage of information.

In the additive secret sharing MPC scheme that we use, all computations are done on integers modulo q, i.e., in a ring $\mathbb{Z}_q = \{0, 1, \ldots, q-1\}$. To map real numbers, such as the trained CNN model parameters, into this ring, we use a fixed point representation with 16 bits of precision for the mantissa. A value x is secret-shared over $\mathbb{Z}_q$ between parties Alice and Bob by picking $x_A, x_B \in \mathbb{Z}_q$ uniformly at random subject to the constraint that $x = x_A + x_B \mod q$, and then revealing x_A to Alice and x_B to Bob. We denote this secret sharing by $[\![x]\!]$, which can be thought of as a shorthand for (x_A, x_B).

Secret-sharing based MPC works by first having the parties split their respective data in secret shares and send some of these shares to each other. To any individual party, their shares of x look like random noise. Only when all of the shares are combined together is the true value of x revealed.

When Alice and Bob have secret-shared numbers $[\![x]\!]$ and $[\![y]\!]$, they can straightforwardly compute $[\![x+y]\!]$ by adding their own shares. To compute $[\![x \cdot y]\!]$, Alice and Bob run a secure multiplication protocol π_{mul} that requires communication between the parties, using a well-known technique with Beaver Triples (Beaver, 1997). These triples can be generated by a trusted initializer (TI) that distributes correlated randomness to Alice and Bob and otherwise does not participate in the computations at all. This is the technique used in CrypTen (Knott et al., 2020) and adopted in the experiments in Sec. 4. Such a TI can be thought of as a third party, next to Alice and Bob, making the setting used in our experiments effectively a three-party configuration. In case a TI is not available or desirable, the required triples can be pre-computed by Alice and Bob in an online phase using an MPC protocol to emulate the TI (Damgård et al., 2012); this method is currently not yet supported in CrypTen.

Building on the cryptographic primitives for addition and multiplication, MPC protocols for other operations have been developed in the literature, many of which we use in turn to build our protocol π_{TEXT}. Of note is the secure comparison protocol π_{comp}, which works by computing the difference of two secret-shared numbers $[\![x]\!]$ and $[\![y]\!]$ and extracting the most significant bit, effectively returning $[\![1]\!]$ if $x < y$, and $[\![0]\!]$ otherwise (more details in (Knott et al., 2020)).

MPC Protocol π_{TEXT}. At the start of the protocol for private text classification, Alice has a CNN model with trained model parameters F, and Bob has an embedding vector D of his text obtained after preprocessing.

- Bob secret-shares vector D with Alice
- Alice secret-shares CNN parameters F with Bob
- Alice and Bob jointly perform computations on the secret sharings $[\![F]\!]$ and $[\![D]\!]$, following the computational graph of $[\![F]\!]$ on $[\![D]\!]$. To this end, for each operation on each layer of the CNN, Alice and Bob execute the appropriate MPC subprotocols, which include:
  - π_{Conv1D}: This operation reduces to the multiplication of secret-shared filter weights with secret-shared input values, and is thus trivially implemented with π_{mul}.
  - $\pi_{MaxPool1D}$: The MaxPool operation is performed through pairwise comparisons with π_{comp} of secret-shared values in a tournament style to determine secret shares of the maximum value for each window.
  - π_{ReLU}: Alice and Bob compute the ReLU activation function of a secret-shared number $[\![x]\!]$ by computing $\pi_{mult}([\![x]\!], \pi_{comp}([\![x]\!], 0))$.
  - π_{Dense}: Application of dense layers reduces to multiplication of matrices with secret-shared numbers, which is an extension of π_{mul}.
  - $\pi_{Sigmoid}$: Alice and Bob compute the sigmoid activation function of a secret-shared number $[\![x]\!]$ using the approximation described by (Knott et al., 2020).
- Alice and Bob execute π_{comp} on the secret-shared output of the CNN to obtain secret shares of the class label.

4 Results

We implemented π_{TEXT} in CrypTen, taking advantage of CrypTen's architecture, which allows to overwrite Torch functions with MPC protocols. All subprotocols needed for π_{TEXT} already existed in the branch crypten-v0.1, barring the π_{Conv1D} and $\pi_{MaxPool1D}$ protocols. We ported π_{Conv1D} from the master branch of CrypTen, and we constructed $\pi_{MaxPool1D}$ ourselves.

In our tests, using $\pi_{Sigmoid}$ to approximate the Sigmoid function made no statistically significant impact on the accuracies. On a test set containing 20,417 instances, using $\pi_{Sigmoid}$ resulted in 17,351 correct classifications, whereas its plaintext counterpart provided 17,350 correct classifications, i.e. an accuracy of 85% across the line. In other words, our use of MPC does not cause accuracy loss. The code we used to run our tests is located on our fork of the CrypTen repository,[2] on the branch "crypten-v0.1".

For our tests, we set up three VMs on Azure, namely one for Alice, one for Bob, and one for the TI. The VMs are Standard L16s_v2, with 16 vCPUs, 128 GiB memory, and an expected network bandwidth of 6400 Mbps. In our experiments, despite having access to large amounts of memory, the parties never used more than 5 GiB at a time.

The TI never sees Alice's or Bob's data. Since the TI's activities are independent of the data that is used as input for the MPC protocols, MPC protocols can be separated in an off-line phase – during which the TI generates correlated randomness and distributes it to Alice and Bob – and an online

[2] `https://github.com/SamuelDAdams/CrypTen`

L16s: Private Text Classifier Runtimes		
# Instances	Sequential (sec)	Batched (sec)
200	151	21
400	296	44
600	445	65
800	596	88
1000	734	110

Table 2: Runtime results (in seconds) to privately classify "#Instances" using π_{TEXT} on Standard L16s_v2 VMs. "Sequential" denotes the protocol is run one instance at a time, and "Batched" shows the runtime to classify all instances in a single batch. All results are an average over 5 runs.

phase – during which Alice and Bob execute the MPC protocols. In CrypTen this separation is not made, hence the results in Tab. 2 include both the offline and the online phase.

Tab. 2 shows the runtime results of π_{TEXT} when privately classifying various amounts of instances (texts). On average, it takes roughly 0.74 seconds to classify a single instance using the sequential method, and 0.11 seconds using the batching method. Batching the classification task outperforms classifying data sequentially by a wide margin. This is because when batching, the parties can also batch communication rounds during the protocol execution, reducing the communication complexity. The time it takes to classify text is reasonably low, and would lend itself to real life applications, showing that MPC-based private text classification with deep learning models is feasible in practice.

5 Conclusion and Future Work

We have presented and evaluated the first application of MPC-based privacy-preserving text classification with CNNs. Our solution involves model owner Alice, who has a multi-channel CNN for text classification, and text owner Bob who transforms his text into an embedding vector using a publicly available BERT model. Next Alice and Bob secret share their inputs and run an MPC protocol to label Bob's text with Alice's model in a provably privacy-preserving manner. Our protocol takes ~ 0.74 sec to classify a text when run in sequential mode, and ~ 0.11 sec when run in batch mode on Standard L16s_v2 Azure virtual machines with an expected bandwidth of 6400 Mbps. These runtimes are independent of the length of the text, as the embedding vector has a fixed length.

Our work serves as a baseline for MPC-based text classification with deep learning that can be improved upon in many ways. From an NLP point of view, we have assumed that Bob can preprocess his text based on public knowledge, in particular with a sentence transformer model that is in no way dependent on Alice's training data or model parameters. While many text preprocessing algorithms are standard and publicly available to all parties (e.g. for stemming, tokenization, etc.), others may involve proprietary information. Pre-trained versions of language representation models that are publicly available can for instance be fine-tuned by model builders (such as Alice) on task specific data, leading to proprietary word or sentence embedding models that the model owners would not want to disclose. The development of effective and efficient MPC protocols for converting raw text into embedding vectors with state-of-the-art transformer architectures is an open problem.

From a security perspective, there exist a variety of MPC schemes beyond the one we considered in this paper, designed for different numbers of parties and offering various level of security that correspond to different threat models and come with different computational costs. Regarding threat models, besides honest-but-curious adversaries, there exist MPC schemes that protect against malicious adversaries that corrupt parties to deviate from the protocol instructions. Regarding the *number* of parties, some of the most efficient MPC schemes have been developed for three computing servers, out of which at most one is corrupted (i.e. honest majority) by an honest-but-curious or a malicious adversary. While text classification is inherently a (dishonest majority) two-party computation problem between the model owner Alice and the text owner Bob, MLaaS (machine learning as a service) set-ups in which Alice and Bob secret share with, and outsource the computations to, three servers in the cloud are growing in popularity in the privacy-preserving ML literature because of their efficiency (Dalskov et al., 2020; Kumar et al., 2020; Riazi et al., 2018; Wagh et al., 2019; Patra and Suresh, 2020). The use of these different MPC schemes for privacy-preserving text classification is an interesting direction for future work.

Acknowledgements. The authors thank Microsoft for the generous donation of cloud computing credits through the UW Azure Cloud Computing Credits for Research program.

References

Nitin Agrawal, Ali Shahin Shamsabadi, Matt J Kusner, and Adrià Gascón. 2019. QUOTIENT: two-party secure neural network training and prediction. In *ACM SIGSAC Conference on Computer and Communications Security*, pages 1231–1247.

Donald Beaver. 1997. Commodity-based cryptography. In *Proceedings of the Twenty-ninth Annual ACM Symposium on Theory of Computing*, STOC '97, pages 446–455.

John Canny. 2002. Collaborative filtering with privacy. In *Proceedings of 2002 IEEE Symposium on Security and Privacy*, pages 45–57.

Nicholas Carlini, Chang Liu, Úlfar Erlingsson, Jernej Kos, and Dawn Song. 2019. The secret sharer: Evaluating and testing unintended memorization in neural networks. In *28th USENIX Security Symposium*, pages 267–284.

Ronald Cramer, Ivan Damgard, and Jesper Nielsen. 2015. *Secure Multiparty Computation and Secret Sharing*. Cambridge University Press.

Anders Dalskov, Daniel Escudero, and Marcel Keller. 2020. Secure evaluation of quantized neural networks. *Proceedings on Privacy Enhancing Technologies*, 2020(4):355–375.

Ivan Damgård, Valerio Pastro, Nigel Smart, and Sarah Zakarias. 2012. Multiparty computation from somewhat homomorphic encryption. In *Annual Cryptology Conference*, pages 643–662. Springer.

David Evans, Vladimir Kolesnikov, and Mike Rosulek. 2018. A pragmatic introduction to secure multi-party computation. *Foundations and Trends in Privacy and Security*, 2(2-3):70–246.

Chiraag Juvekar, Vinod Vaikuntanathan, and Anantha Chandrakasan. 2018. GAZELLE: A low latency framework for secure neural network inference. In *27th USENIX Security Symposium*, pages 1651–1669.

Yoon Kim. 2014. Convolutional neural networks for sentence classification. In *Proceedings of the 2014 Conference on Empirical Methods in Natural Language Processing (EMNLP)*, pages 1746–1751.

Brian Knott, Shobha Venkataraman, Awni Hannun, Shubho Sengupta, Mark Ibrahim, and Laurens van der Maaten. 2020. CrypTen: Secure multi-party computation meets machine learning. In *NeurIPS Workshop on Privacy-Preserving Machine Learning*.

Nishant Kumar, Mayank Rathee, Nishanth Chandran, Divya Gupta, Aseem Rastogi, and Rahul Sharma. 2020. CrypTFlow: Secure TensorFlow inference. In *41st IEEE Symposium on Security and Privacy*, pages 336–353.

Pratyush Mishra, Ryan Lehmkuhl, Akshayaram Srinivasan, Wenting Zheng, and Raluca Ada Popa. 2020. Delphi: A cryptographic inference service for neural networks. In *29th USENIX Security Symposium*, pages 2505–2522.

Arpita Patra and Ajith Suresh. 2020. BLAZE: Blazing fast privacy-preserving machine learning. *arXiv preprint arXiv:2005.09042*.

Devin Reich, Ariel Todoki, Rafael Dowsley, Martine De Cock, and Anderson Nascimento. 2019. Privacy-preserving classification of personal text messages with secure multi-party computation. In *Advances in Neural Information Processing Systems (NeurIPS)*, pages 3752–3764.

Nils Reimers and Iryna Gurevych. 2019. Sentence-bert: Sentence embeddings using siamese bert-networks. In *Proceedings of the 2019 Conference on Empirical Methods in Natural Language Processing and the 9th International Joint Conference on Natural Language Processing (EMNLP-IJCNLP)*, pages 3973–3983.

Amanda Resende, Davis Railsback, Rafael Dowsley, Anderson C. A. Nascimento, and Diego F. Aranha. 2021. Fast privacy-preserving text classification based on secure multiparty computation. Cryptology ePrint Archive, Report 2021/069.

M. Sadegh Riazi, Christian Weinert, Oleksandr Tkachenko, Ebrahim M. Songhori, Thomas Schneider, and Farinaz Koushanfar. 2018. Chameleon: A hybrid secure computation framework for machine learning applications. In *Asia Conference on Computer and Communications Security*, pages 707–721.

Olivia Solon. 2018. Facebook says Cambridge Analytica may have gained 37M more users' data. *The Guardian*, Apr 4.

Stuart A. Thompson and Charlie Warzel. 2019. Twelve million phones, one dataset, zero privacy. *The New York Times*, Dec 19.

Sameer Wagh, Divya Gupta, and Nishanth Chandran. 2019. SecureNN: 3-party secure computation for neural network training. *Proceedings on Privacy Enhancing Technologies*, 2019(3):26–49.

Author Index

Association for Computational Linguistics
209 N. Eighth Street
Stroudsburg, Pennsylvania 18360

ISBN 978-1-7138-3026-9

CURRAN ASSOCIATES INC.
proceedings.com